LEASE–PURCHASE
America!

John Ross

LEASE–PURCHASE
America!

John Ross

STARBURST PUBLISHERS

P.O. Box 4123, Lancaster, Pennsylvania 17604

John Ross has spent the last 12 years learning real estate literally "from the ground up." John is a respected entrepreneur and travels throughout North America for consulting and speaking engagements. He also conducts seminars, workshops, and educational retreats—as well as management and staff training for major U.S. corporations. John's experience and his popularity as a speaker have combined to help him become the country's leading expert on lease-purchase real estate. In 1991 he received an achievement award from *Success Magazine* and is the author of *Rags To Riches to Rags To Riches*.

To schedule Author appearances write:
Author Appearances, Starburst Promotions, P.O. Box 4123
Lancaster, Pennsylvania 17604 or call (717) 293-0939.

Credits:
Cover art by Bill Dussinger.

LEASE–PURCHASE AMERICA!

First Printing, December 1993

ISBN: 0-914984-45-4
Library of Congress Catalog Number 92-81393
Printed in the United States of America

I wish to thank . . .

My Heavenly Father for giving me a second chance in life and all the blessings He generously bestows upon me;

My children Lia, Kevin, Jeffrey, and Janelle for bringing such fullness and joy into my life;

My wife, partner, and best friend Kelly Kay, for loving me from the first moment we saw each other, and for caring for me like an angel;

Rob Simpson for truly being my "best man" over all the years we have known each other;

Bill Taaffe for telling me over and over again that "I have magic," and for believing in me from the beginning;

The many people who have believed in me, continue to believe in me, and give me their support.

Comments

"The Lease-Purchase System for the '90s complies with provisions, and has been duly accepted and approved as real estate continuing education for Realtors."

Georgia Real Estate Commission

"Thank you for all you've done. The staff and youth were inspired and amazed by your expertise. You infuse a positive self-image in all you do, and I can see a difference in people already."

Pat Sullivan, The Salvation Army

"During the '80s I made a lot of money by wheeling and dealing in real estate. Unfortunately, the crash came. After reading about your concepts, it revitalized my ambitions and convictions to succeed. I thank you for going public with your innovative lease-purchase ideas; I am sure there are thousands of people out there like me who can benefit and need to hear them."

Ray Quiles, Realtor - ERA

"The secrets of your Lease-Purchase program are most important. Your program, by far, is the most realistic for today's economy. I was blessed to have crossed paths with you and see the opportunity."

Larry Lawrence, Federal Express Corporation

John is an outstanding professional with a superb program. It is certainly of interest to our people. He is a dynamic and experienced real estate expert. This is the best strategy we've seen for these times."

James Reef - Charles J. Givens Group, NJ Chapter

"This lease-purchase concept is the best way I've seen for an individual to be involved with properties and make real cash today. Whether you're a Realtor or an investor, lease-purchase is THE way of the '90s."

Carlos Rivera, Realtor of the Year - ReMax Atlanta

"We started using John's lease-purchase concept and within a week found our ideal home and moved in! Lease-purchase helped us to make a move quick. We are 100% satisfied. We recommend the method to anyone buying a home."

Jackie & Bob Edwards, Small Business Entrepreneurs

"I never thought I could own a home, and without lease-purchase, I'd still be renting. The unique opportunity of lease-purchase has allowed me to own a home with monthly payments equivalent to renting. Now I've got all the benefits of home ownership, and my money is working for me. Thanks to you and lease-purchase, I'm no longer throwing money out the window each month on rent!"

Chakaris Moss, Psychiatrist

"John, your lease-purchase concept is most interesting and informative. It has given us as owners, and our staff, the nuts and bolts we need to proceed in our business. Your book is straightforward yet comprehensive. We've already had success with it and can see our way clear to doing a great deal more. We appreciate your opening the world of lease-purchasing to us."

Bernard Weiss, Broker/Owner - Century 21-Best Realty, New York

"As professionals in the ever-changing real estate industry, our knowledge is never complete. Your information is very useful and your ideas have brought new life to the industry."

Laura Mahoney, Chairman - Young Council of Realtors

"Within just one month, I've been able to put together two lease-purchase deals amounting to more than $3,000 in cash profit in my pocket with only a few hours work a week. The numbers you described in your book are proving correct and coming true."

Marvin Johnson, President - Fortune Financial Consultants

"I can't thank you enough for all the knowledge and experience you've shared via your lease-purchase techniques. Your passion, knowledge, and enthusiasm for real estate using lease-purchase is incredible. What I've learned is easily adaptable to my life—I can put it to use immediately."

Sean Rasmus, President - Rasmus Construction, Inc.

"Lease-purchase is a great introduction into the real estate arena. John, your concepts have proven to be some of the most innovative, exciting, and enlightening pieces of information in my educational arsenal."

John V. Bailey III, Boutique Owner/Property Investor

"Your knowledge in real estate is exceptional. The material you've provided in your lease-purchase book is easy to understand. The information seems to be tailored specifically to my needs and the current market. Anyone can practice this information you teach and grow from it financially. The time spent with your techniques was probably the most valuable time I've spent as long as I can remember. I thank God for this opportunity."

Gregory P. Gosselin, Partner - Rojac Company, Inc.

"This is a tremendously interesting and timely concept for anyone who is buying or selling homes. John delivers his message with charisma."

Queenie Collins, Assistant Vice President - Georgia Federal Bank

"This is an idea that is revolutionizing the real estate market throughout the country."

Real Estate Leadership Association of America

"Your contribution to our audience was tremendous. The amount of education you brought to our attention was timely and streamlined for the '90s. Your concepts and ideas were informative and enlightening."

Christopher Ervin, CEO - Community Forum

"Thank you so much. I've had many inquiries about your book and your availability to lecture on your lease-purchase concept. We want you to come back for another show and talk more about lease-purchase—our audience is thirsting for this information."

Jordan Graye, WSB-FM Radio, Atlanta

Table of Contents

1

Introduction

Why I wrote this book.

I wrote *Lease-Purchase, America!* with one goal in mind: to help you buy a home,

Or sell a home,

Or invest in a property.

It's really that simple.

My goal is to make real estate affordable and available to everyone—using a method that is as simple as it is straightforward, and that benefits all parties equally in the process.

I am a survivor of the '80s real estate craze . . . and crash. If you are too, you may have realized the same truths that I did. First, yesterday's methods don't work in today's market.

Second, the "get-rich-quick" methods that are still hyped by the late-night TV gurus work to make only one person get-rich-quick—themselves!

When you look more closely at the "get-rich-quick" real estate tactics you see that they are a lot like playing the lottery. Sure, the payoff can be big. But think about it . . . realistically. What *are* your chances of hitting the winning ticket? One in a million? Or worse?

Would you bet your next paycheck on that chance?

And what happens when you *don't* win?

Those are not the odds you're willing to risk when it comes to making a living. Or to get yourself into a home.

Of course, it's not just a matter of luck. The price of real estate and a temperamental economy still make owning a home difficult for the average person. And almost impossible for young couples, especially those just entering the work force.

Don't get me wrong. I *believe* in the "American Dream" of owning a home.

That's why I started looking for a method that would let the average person buy a home with as little money down as possible, and that was still fair to buyer and seller. Unlike the "gurus," I wasn't looking for shortcuts to make a fortune overnight; I just wanted to purchase a home after having to start over again—and to begin generating a realistic income.

In other words, I needed something I could live on . . . and that my conscience could live with!

What I found was lease-purchase.

No, the concept of lease-purchase isn't new. In fact, it has been a major force for years in the billion-dollar rent-to-own industry. We've seen "rent-to-own" audio/video gear, appliances, furniture, and more. More recently, the automobile industry has followed suit with varied lease-to-own programs.

So why not real estate?

I look at lease-purchase as a fresh, new, and common-sense method of buying or selling your next home or investment property. It's logical, it's simple, it's legal, and it works.

Best of all, it's an idea that is exploding throughout the real estate world.

With the dramatic changes that have occurred in tax laws and the real estate marketplace, lease-purchase has become (and will continue to be) a vital part of real estate throughout this decade.

So let's talk for a minute about this book.

Although I had found this great technique that fit my needs, what I could *not* find were experts that taught how to use lease-purchase to buy properties. Nor could I find any books that clearly outlined a simple, workable program for lease-purchase.

So I decided to write one.

Lease–Purchase, America! should be required reading for anyone who is ever going to buy, sell, or rent a home. These techniques are based on my own experiences developing the program from scratch over a multi-year period.

Lease-Purchase, America! will explain for you, in clear-cut fashion, how lease-purchase provides an alternative to anyone who has wanted to buy a home but couldn't due to insufficient cash, credit problems, or inexperience in the real estate market.

You'll also learn, step by step, how to acquire a property with this realistic and sensible system that differs greatly from the "no-money-down" theories that ran rampant in the '80s.

And you'll learn why lease-purchase represents such an attractive alternative to the buyer who may not be able to afford a home, as well as to the seller who may not have been able to sell a home.

Lease-purchase is a valuable tool whether you're on the buying or selling side of the table. Actually, it puts buyer and seller on the same side of the table. . . helping you arrive at a deal where both parties benefit. It's called, "win-win."

And "win-win" is something you don't hear of very often in real estate!

In short, *Lease–Purchase, America!* is designed specifically to help:

- the first-time home buyer/renter to get his or her first home; or
- the seller who has been unable to sell his or her property.

Of course, by employing exactly the same principles, this technique also will benefit:

- the beginning investor to obtain his first property;
- the investor who needs a new realistic approach to property acquisition; and
- the business person who wants to invest.

Now, you're probably asking yourself, "Why should I listen to this person?"

That's a fair question. It's one I would ask if I were in your shoes.

But I think I can give you some pretty good reasons.

2

Trial by fire

Who is John Ross?

I'd rather not tell you this story. Even after many years, it's still not easy to share.

But it's important that you read it.

That's because when you understand where I've been, I believe you'll better understand how my experience can help you become more successful, and more satisfied, with your real estate acquisitions.

As I said earlier, I survived the '80s real estate craze. But just barely. Because it was during the '80s that I made an incredible fortune and, almost overnight, saw everything taken away from me with four little words that almost destroyed my life: "You are under arrest."

Perhaps I should start at the beginning.

I bought my first home in 1982. It was a small, single-family house in upstate New York that I bought for $23,500; the sellers agreed to pay closing costs and points. I was approved for a 95% conventional loan and came up with the down payment with a cash advance from my MasterCard.

At closing, the seller rebated back to me $2,500 for a "decorator allowance."

This meant that, not only was I able to buy the home with no money out of my pocket, but I also received money at closing to fix it up.

I used that money to put on a new roof, paint inside and out, and install new kitchen cabinets and flooring. Three months after I bought the home, I went back to the bank for refinancing.

The bank appraised the home for $40,000, and gave me an 85% "loan to value." With the new $34,000 loan, I paid off the first loan and had more than $10,000 in tax-deferred cash.

I was hooked.

This was my first taste of real estate, and I knew I could do it again, just as easily. I decided that if my second deal turned out as well as the first, I would do this full-time. After all, I had no experience—and still made money. With hard work, I believed I could make a fortune.

Although I still had a full-time job selling insurance, I jumped into real estate with the same unbridled energy I applied to everything else in my life. I continued buying, fixing up, and either selling, refinancing, or renting properties.

It was a gold mine.

By working hard and being smart, I found that I could "flip" properties (turn and sell them almost immediately) and make big profits in a short period of time. On one property, I netted a $60,000 profit in two months. It didn't take me long to realize that I could make a living doing this!

Within a year, I had quit my job and went into real estate investing full-time. I hired a full-time foreman to manage the property renovations; we were on our way.

My career took off. I brought partners and investors into projects. I did ten to twenty deals each month. And I began to build a staff and an office.

During this period of rapid success, I learned an interesting principle: nothing is ever perfect and, if you wait for perfection, you'll spend the rest of your life waiting.

A good friend and I would analyze properties together. I would buy, but he would hesitate, because none seemed perfect enough for him. His approach was much like one described by Zig Ziglar: "Some people won't back out of their driveways to go on a trip until all the lights are green."

My friend suffered from "paralysis of analysis." He was paralyzed into inaction by a desire to know too much. He wanted all the lights to be green. I didn't. So I made a fortune. And he's still waiting.

My company was called J. Ross Development. As my business expanded, I hired more and more people to keep up with the work.

Eventually I had a large staff, including my own full-time attorney and accountant, two rehab crews, and a management division.

As my company grew, I found that the only thing holding me back was cash; with more cash, my business could grow faster than ever.

My new attorney introduced me to the top manager for the area's largest real estate and mortgage brokerage firm. A few days and dinners later, this gentleman and his firm extended to me a $250,000 line of credit.

It was perfect. I could walk into the broker's office, give his secretary a copy of the purchase offer for a property, explain how much money I needed for repairs—and walk out with a check. My business really started to take off!

Because of my rather sudden rise from rags to riches, I became a kind of local celebrity.

I found myself appearing on a number of TV and radio talk shows, and was featured in newspaper and magazine articles. I was even asked to write a weekly real estate investment column. Life was good.

I want to point out that, as good as my professional life was, my home life was better. I had a wonderful family and saw it grow to include four beautiful children.

Even though I worked hard, I always had time for my family. I was there when each child rolled over for the first time. I saw their first steps and heard their first words. I even helped each of them ride a bike for the first time.

As I began doing well financially, I even planned my career around my children. I worked only during school hours. I dropped them off and picked them up from school. We planned weekly outings. We had fun.

I loved being a father. And my wife was a great mother.

My life, both professionally and privately, was better than any fairy tale I could have imagined: "And they lived happily ever after."

After all, I had built a personal net worth of $1.2 million. In the process, I had created a thriving, successful business. I loved what I was doing. I had everything I had ever dreamed of.

And then my dream turned into a nightmare.

In exchange for the $250,000 line of credit, I had given the broker in New York a blanket mortgage on 22 of my properties. In addition, I had pledged more than $750,000 in other mortgages, because I wanted him to increase my credit limit as soon as possible.

The line of credit was a 90-day demand note, and the brokerage company assured me that they would work with me to "roll over" the notes if I couldn't pay them in full.

At first, everything went well.

Ninety days after the first note, I was prepared to pay principle and interest in full, but I was told that I only needed to pay the interest. So I did. I then went and bought four more properties for cash, investing the principle for a better return.

Then, the market dropped.

When the note came due again, the broker demanded payment in full. I asked for time to sell my properties, but that was refused. Instead, the brokerage firm suggested that their agents sell the properties (for less than 80 percent of their value). That would have cost me a fortune, so I begged for more time. Again, my request was denied.

I had ten days to raise $250,000. And everything was on the line.

I went to bank after bank, but kept running into dead ends. I scrambled like never before.

Suddenly, my time was up.

With the note called due, I was forced into bankruptcy—both as a corporation *and* personally.

All my properties were gone. I lost millions, and many of my clients ended up losing the money they had invested jointly in properties.

But I didn't quit.

Rather than lament my losses, I decided to rebuild my fortune and make things right with anyone who may have been financially hurt by my setback.

I established another corporation, called Check Mate Realty. My employees stayed with me. And I found two investors who provided seed money to get things going again. So, once again, we were on our way.

I hid nothing about my misfortune from the investors or my employees. I found that they appreciated my candor and, rather than being put off by the experience, trusted me all the more.

With the new company, I changed the structure a bit so that I did not take title to properties. Instead, I was paid a "finder's fee" for locating properties. I also was paid to fix them up and, finally, I received a percentage after they were sold.

It was a good plan.

All in all, things were looking up. I began to make money again. And I completed preparations begun months before to expand the business by opening an office in Atlanta, Georgia.

I remember thinking, "The hard part is over. I think we're going to make it!"

I was wrong.

Three days before we were scheduled to move to Atlanta, two men walked into my office. Their dark suits looked out of place, especially in the warm July sun.

"Mr. Ross, we're with the FBI. You are under arrest."

At that instant, time froze. I was caught in an explosion of still-frame images of my past 28 years. Childhood games. Sitting with my wife and children at church. Seeing my dreams come to life, one by one. Then pulled apart by bankruptcy.

And now this.

Slowly, I forced myself back to reality—this was 1988, and it was not a dream. I stood and walked out of my office between the two men.

I learned that some of my former clients had filed criminal charges against me because of my bankruptcy. They *actually* had convinced themselves that I had intentionally set up the bankruptcy.

Personally, I think they had been watching too much TV.

Because of the arrest, I sat and waited in jail, charged with ten counts of grand larceny. Bail was set at $50,000. It was my mother who put up bail, offering her house as collateral.

Jail left me with a lasting impression of the human spirit we often fail to recognize when we are behind bars. The guards and the inmates treated me with kindness and compassion. Before I left, I vowed that I would repay them someday. Somehow.

But at the moment, I was facing a maximum 88-year sentence. I needed help.

I tried, unsuccessfully, to retain counsel. It was apparent that the press had done such a good job of covering the story that no one wanted anything to do with me.

Finally, I was referred to a successful and competent criminal attorney who at first, like the others, was not willing to take my case. But he agreed to listen to me for 15 minutes.

After I explained what had happened, the attorney was furious. He told me that the charges were ridiculous and then agreed to take my case.

But money was a problem; the legal fees were expected to exceed $25,000. And I was broke!

Again, my mother stepped in.

Using part of the life insurance benefit she received from my father's death, she offered to pay the legal fees.

My wife and I decided to go ahead with our move to Atlanta. I was unable to leave New York without the court's approval, so she and the children went on ahead with the understanding that I would go to them as soon as possible.

I didn't want my family to leave me, but I knew it was best for them. They needed to get into a new home where they could feel secure and where we could start over.

"Starting over" was doubly important, because my wife and I were having marital problems even before the stress of the bankruptcy. We had married young and were two very different people, with only our church and our children in common. For months, we had been going to marriage counselors to improve our relationship. It wasn't working.

We needed a change.

It was three weeks before I received permission to leave New York. Those were twenty-one hectic days spent meeting with the attorney and tying up the loose ends of my second collapsed business.

I finally arrived in Atlanta—broke, without a business or a job, and with an upcoming court case that could put me in prison for the rest of my life.

But I couldn't afford the luxury of licking my wounds. After all, I had a family to feed.

With a criminal case pending, I knew I couldn't get back into real estate. Not yet. But I knew I could sell, so I vigorously scanned the newspapers for any opportunity.

After interviewing with many "shady" companies and even more less-than-impressive managers, I found a solid company that manufactured and sold water filters. Quite a departure from real estate, but it was a good product, and I knew I could sell it. And the company offered a multi-level program, so the income potential was fairly open-ended.

I began selling door-to-door—a sales technique with which I was *very* familiar! I concentrated on selling, rather than building a multi-level organization. And I did fairly well, although I did not make the kind of money that I had hoped for. But I stayed with it until my case came to court—which was almost a full year after my move to Atlanta.

I don't have to tell you that this was a tough time for me. Even though I had spent my entire life focused on maintaining a positive mental attitude, I fought despair every single day. Friends assured me that the case would be dismissed; still, the idea of an 88-year prison term weighed heavily on my mind.

The strain took its toll. My relationship with my wife deteriorated further. We shared the same house, our children, but nothing else. It wasn't long before we were divorced.

It was during this same period that my mother died. She had been a constant friend and provided support when everyone else turned their backs on me. We were very close, and her death broke my heart.

I don't think I could have imagined worse pain. I had truly lost everything: my marriage, my family, my friends, my wealth. I was left with nothing but a grim determination to "hang on."

Finally, in May 1989, my case was scheduled for court. I flew to New York and anxiously waited for an end to the nightmare.

Or the beginning of another?

When my name was read in court, I approached the bench. Opening statements were made. The judge nodded and shook his head.

In less than fifteen minutes, after a year of waiting, it was over.

The judge echoed the words of my attorney when he said that the charges were *ludicrous*. He added that my case should never have come to trial. Then he told me something that opened my eyes and my heart:

He told me that I had to start over.

The judge talked to me as a father might give personal counsel to his son. He told me to go, and to leave behind the heavy burden of bitterness and malice.

He admonished me to rebuild my life without getting caught up in crippling feelings of vengeance against the people who had unjustly accused me, and against the system that had allowed things to go as far as they did. He added that such negative feelings would destroy me if I let them.

Although the situation was unfortunate, he said I had no choice but to start over.

I appreciated the judge's counsel. I'd like to believe that I would not have allowed myself to become tangled in negative feelings about the past, but his warning helped me watch out for them.

Starting over turned out to be the best thing I ever did.

With the baggage of false criminal charges lifted, I was ready to get back into real estate. I wanted to get into a home and, finally, put down some roots.

And I wanted a way to make money. Again.

Because of my cash-poor situation, I needed to find a process that was simple enough that it could be repeated, that avoided a great deal of negotiating and could be done without cash or credit.

I was looking for something that was as simple as renting an apartment, and yet offered greater profit potential.

That turned out to be **lease-purchase.**

Although I knew nothing about lease-purchase, it didn't take me long to learn. With the financial help of a local investor, I began negotiating lease-purchase deals betwen buyers and sellers.

With each transaction I completed, I more clearly saw the vast potential for buyers, sellers, real estate brokers, and investors. I was amazed. Unlike the other real estate techniques I had tried in the past, lease-purchase was truly a win-win situation for everyone. No matter which hat I wore in a transaction, I benefited.

My initial success with lease-purchase led me into doing deals for myself and perpetuating my business.

I was even able to get *myself* a home, thanks to lease-purchase.

I was impressed. Lease-purchase was equitable. It worked!

I knew I had found another winner.

Still, I was amazed that more and more people were *not* using this incredible technique to by or sell their homes.

Especially when I saw homes sitting on the market month after month.

That's when I realized that people simply didn't understand how well (and how simply) lease-purchase could work for them. But I knew I could teach them.

I was on my way. The rest, as they say, is history.

And fortunately, for me, that history is still being written!

3

It's not the same "song and dance" anymore

*The complexion of real estate—
and investing—has changed dramatically.
And it continues to evolve.*

I bought my first home in the early '80s.

That was during a time when you could basically buy a home without any idea what you were doing and still get a good deal. Properties were appreciating somewhere in the range of 2 to 5 percent, and just holding onto any property seemed to work well.

For the investors, the solid appreciation of homes, as well as the accelerated depreciation allowed by the tax system, combined to make single family homes a fabulous investment. The economy was good and money was prevalent. You could borrow and refinance with ease.

I knew many people who were able to buy homes under FHA with nothing coming out of their own pockets. And owner-financing deals were available on a regular basis. All you had to do was look in the classified "For Sale" or "For Rent" section of any newspaper.

Even banks were riding the real estate bandwagon. Banks had not gone through the disasters that have occurred in the last several years. Foreclosures were not as prevalent.

Now, everyone seems to be running around scared and overly cautious. Banks have tightened up severely. In fact, a recent article in *USA Today* reported that a number of banks were placing a significant portion of their lendable assets into treasury notes, rather than into consumer lending, to take advantage of higher returns and lower risk.

The result is that we are having a more difficult time trying to buy and sell properties, and to obtain loans.

There's no question: money is tight. Period.

The economy is struggling. The entire banking industry is going through a tremendous upheaval. Properties are not appreciating like they used to. From coast to coast the market has changed dramatically.

And one of the most influential changes has come as a direct result of the spending habits of the American people.

That's why it's interesting to note that the rent-to-own industry also began to flourish in the '80s. Rent-to-own furniture was a new concept that satisfied a "niche" in the marketplace. It quickly caught on, fed by our changing habits.

To understand the power of rent-to-own, first understand one absolute truth about our society:

We want it now!

Years ago, people used to scrimp and save and make do with what they had until they could afford to pay cash. Today, we have evolved into a "get it now and pay for it later" credit generation.

Just open any Sunday circular and you'll see. Ads with big, bold headlines that proclaim, "Buy it now. Pay later." "No payments until next year." And more.

People have been conditioned to spend . . . and extend . . . their money.

Because of that, people simply don't have money saved for the important things, like buying a home.

Sure, people are able to make monthly payments, but they can't afford down payments. Paying even an extra few hundred dollars per month seems to work easier than saving up the necessary down payment money needed to purchase many durable goods in the marketplace.

Therefore, it has been a natural process to see the rent-to-own concept move from smaller priced items like appliances, stereos, and televisions . . . on to furniture, then automobiles and airplanes . . . and now *homes*!

But keep in mind that this trend is not necessarily bad. In fact, it is better to put your "rent to own" money into a home than spend it on anything else!

Half the people who want to buy homes can't because they simply don't have enough cash to make an adequate down payment. Most also have inferior credit (another symptom of our "buy now, pay later" society).

With insufficient cash or credit, these people are simply locked out of the home-buying marketplace.

Lease-purchase is providing a mechanism for change.

Lease-purchase (or lease to own, rent to own, or lease-option, as people have called it in the past) has grown out of a need.

It's a need created by the economy and the spending habits of consumers. (I'll explain this a little more in Chapter 5—we'll talk with some leaders in the "rent to own" industry.)

Now is an appropriate time for this concept to be adopted throughout the residential home ownership market. It is swiftly replacing the "no-money" down techniques of the '80s, since it provides a fair and creative way to benefit everyone involved in the transaction.

And the key word is "fair."

The problem with the '80s mentality and "no money down" was that the seller had to give up title to the buyer . . . and then trust that the buyer would honor the contract and, over time, make the deal worthwhile.

Understandably, that created a tremendous amount of insecurity and vulnerability for the seller.

Imagine giving your car (and title) to a person with the agreement that they would keep up payments on your auto loan. Of course, the loan is still in your name, right? So you've given up the security of the car, and you're at the mercy of the person who has possession (and ownership) of the car to make *your* payments.

And if they don't keep up the payments, who is liable? You are!

You would have to go after them and try to repossess the vehicle. Meanwhile, the bank is coming after *you* for payment.

Not easy, and definitely not fun.

Real estate deals under this scenario suffered similar drawbacks. In fact, the insecurity, the frustration, and the headaches of the legal battles (including repossessions) led many people to abandon this technique.

It is true that thousands of low-down payment (and even nothing-down) deals were done in the past. However, as more and more people became educated and realized the risks of this system (the numbers of foreclosures alone were staggering), this concept of financing and marketing properties slowly died away.

While it is true that the buyer benefits by not having to come up with much money (if any at all), the seller will always be in a poor position. Even when sellers are in dire financial need, they are often afraid of this type of transaction—since they have to give up their title and are left with no security (and no leverage against the buyer).

Today with the lease-purchase concept, sellers are able to perform low-down—and sometimes no-down—deals with comfort because, first and foremost, they get to keep their title!

This one fact reduces (and often totally eliminates) any insecurity about the deal. In essence, the lease-purchase is *just* a lease . . . and later it has the potential to become a purchase.

If the seller is going to hold financing, he will have had payments coming in for a period of time (usually one year) and will feel more comfortable after seeing the buyer develop a proven payment history.

Of course, lease-purchase is not the answer to everyone's problems.

It is however, a positive . . . and powerful . . . alternative to the previous choices available to both buyers and sellers.

Lease-purchase opens doors.

4

What is a Lease–Purchase?

A lease-purchase is a lease combined with a purchase offer:

Lease Contract	+	Purchase Offer Contract	=	Lease–Purchase Agreement (Contract)

The buyer makes payments to a seller in the same way he would if he were renting. However, in a lease-purchase, the payments are called lease-purchase payments. Many times the amount of the payment is the same or similar to a rental payment amount. Usually the seller credits a percentage of the payment towards the purchase price (averages about 20-25%).

The term is typically for one year, although it can be made longer or shorter to meet the needs of both the buyer and the seller.

An amount of money is paid up front and is applied toward the purchase price. This is called an "option consideration"—it usually is about 2 percent of the purchase price. Instead of a rental deposit which is refundable, the option amount is non-refundable.

The purchase price and method of payment is determined at the beginning of the term.

Here's a more formal textbook definition:

A lease-purchase is a process that combines a basic lease with a contract to purchase, or with an option to purchase. The buyer (or the lease-purchaser) pays to the seller a monthly payment that usually approximates a rental amount or the typical mortgage payments on the home. A percentage of that payment is applied toward the purchase price. At the end of the term, the buyer has the right to buy the property under the price and terms to which both parties have previously agreed.

Unlike traditional renting, the lease-purchase buyer is able to apply some of his monthly "rent" to the purchase of the home. And unlike traditional "no money down" deals, the seller is able to retain title to the property until adequate arrangements are made for the actual sale.

In some ways, lease-purchase plans are economically more advantageous than actually owning your home. This is so because, during the first year, more of your monthly payment is applied toward the principal in lease-purchase than is applied using a traditional mortgage.

If and when the lease-purchaser decides to exercise his option to buy, he has several choices. He can come up with a cash payment, negotiate owner financing, get a new loan, or seek financing through an outside investor.

If the buyer comes up with an agreed upon amount of cash—

- (he has the term of the lease-purchase, usually one year, to save the money required to make the down payment)

. . . he may be able to assume an existing loan—unless market prices make assumables difficult—

- (a lease-purchase also gives the seller time to see if the buyer is going to pay on time)

. . . or he can have the owner hold financing.

If payments are made on time during the term of the lease-purchase, the likelihood of some type of owner financing is increased since a good payment history has been established. The major reason you don't see more "no-down" deals is the seller's fear that the buyer will not make his payments and then be forced into foreclosing on him. Since the seller retains title until the option is exercised, he is protected.

Or, the buyer simply can apply for a new loan.

Often, buyers have difficulty qualifying for a new loan because they don't have the necessary down payment. With lease-purchase, the buyers are given time to save additional cash; at the same time, a percentage of their monthly payment is set aside by the seller to be applied to the purchase price. This opens the doors to VA, FHA, and conventional loans for the buyer.

Or, the buyer can arrange outside financing with an investor to pay the difference between the sale price and the amount of the first mortgage (that is assumable or owner-financed).

Also, a buyer may be able to locate private sources of money. . . from family members or through certain investment groups.

My start with lease-purchase

In Atlanta, I found an investor who had a substantial amount of money in certificates of deposit. . . but he wanted a better return on his investment. He wanted to buy homes and then sell them through lease-purchase for a reasonable profit.

We went to work. I helped him find suitable properties, and I negotiated with the sellers and buyers.

In most cases, the lease-purchase contract was written for a one-year term. During that time, the potential buyers paid rent and took care of the property.

After one year, the investor allowed the buyers to come up with a small amount as down payment and he would hold the financing. Some of the homes had assumable loans on them; many didn't. Therefore, he was in a position to act as a bank and collect payments for each and every property.

Here's an example of how the lease-purchase transactions worked:

The investor's purchase price was $75,000. His mortgage payment was $650 per month. This included PITI (principal, interest, taxes, and insurance) on a $60,000 first mortgage at 10 percent.

He would buy the properties by putting approximately $15,000 down on each house. The buyer would then lease-purchase the home from him for one year making payments of $700 per month. The investor credited the buyer $100 per month toward the purchase price.

After one year, the investor (as seller) either allowed the buyer to assume the loan (if one existed), or he would hold financing. Either way, the buyer did not have to come up with more than another $1,000 or $2,000 at the end of the lease-purchase term. This worked out well for the buyers, and it was just as good for the investor.

Sale price	$85,000
Buyer assumes	$60,000
Remaining	$25,000

(The owner would hold $25,000 as a 2nd mortgage, and the buyer made payments directly to the seller.)

In this scenario, the investor made $10,000 per property and the buyer was able to buy a home with only a small down payment in the beginning and a small down payment at the end of the term.

In other words, both were winners.

It wasn't long before I also discovered that one lease-purchase deal would invariably lead to another.

After one of my first lease-purchase deals, the seller was so happy with the way it turned out, he called me a few months later with another property he had purchased and asked me if I wanted to do a lease-purchase on another property.

After analyzing the information on it, I quickly realized this was going to work best as an owner-financed transaction. That's because the seller had paid cash for it and wanted a steady income rather than a lump sum payment.

The strange thing about this situation was the seller had sold the property twice and the buyers did not qualify with the bank. (Why the buyers went for a mortgage, I don't know.) All I knew was the seller was willing to hold financing now and did not require a credit check. He just wanted an income from the property. Instead of leaving his money in a certificate of deposit with a bank, he decided to buy a property and resell it to get a higher interest rate on his money.

This worked out well for the seller and for me.

I was able to buy the property and then lease-purchase it out to someone else. After one year, I allowed the buyers to assume the underlying first mortgage (from the seller), and I held a second mortgage.

My purchase price $83,000
(with $800/month paid to seller)

Mortgage amount $83,000

Resale price $92,000

The buyer paid $2,000 down as option money. I credited $100 of his monthly rent to the purchase price.

At the end of the year, they closed.

The interesting part of this deal was the knowledge I gained knowing that people were becoming more and more interested in lease-purchase. And I learned that, by simply being involved in lease-purchasing of properties, I could find true "deals" that otherwise I never would have heard of.

Lease-Purchase benefits
from everyone's perspective.

As I've said before, lease-purchase is one of the few real estate techniques that offers a "win-win" opportunity for everyone involved.

Now I know that every program professes a similar benefit. But lease-purchase offers advantages to all parties alike: seller, buyer, renter, landlord, real estate agent, and investor.

Let's take a look at lease-purchase from the perspective of each participant. You may notice that some of the benefits overlap, but I want to present a clear idea of the range of advantages the technique offers to each party.

Advantages for the seller

Without question, the primary benefit of a lease-purchase arrangement for the seller is that his house payment or mortgage payment is being covered. He is thus freed financially from the monthly burden of the property during the term of the lease-purchase. In some cases, this arrangement can even mean saving him from foreclosure.

But the seller also may benefit in other ways from a lease-purchase contract. One advantage may come in simply delaying the actual sale of the property. There are numerous cases where sellers have realized tax benefits by delaying closing. Because a lease-purchase delays closing by a year (or more), the seller has additional time to investigate and plan for the tax consequences of the sale . . . and use them to his best advantage.

Another advantage is that, using lease-purchase, the seller is more likely to realize his asking price.

Think of it this way. When you pay cash for something, you naturally might expect a discount. When you buy on credit or delayed payment terms, you understand that you will pay the asking price ("retail"). In some cases, you may even pay a slightly higher price . . . or extra charges . . . to reflect that added service.

The time value of money also comes into the picture. As you know, money today is worth more than money tomorrow.

In a lease-purchase, the seller doesn't receive his full payment immediately and, therefore, cannot make use of his money. Since he is accepting payment in "tomorrow's" dollars, the value of those dollars should be adjusted upwards to compensate.

In many instances, the seller is able to get a higher "rent" or income (in the form of lease-purchase payments) per month since the payments become like a forced savings plan for the buyer.

So, by offering the flexibility of lease-purchase, a seller is actually making his house more immediately affordable and, therefore, a better value in today's market and today's dollars. For that reason, he can fully justify his asking price.

Risk is another benefit. Or, rather, the elimination of risk, because lease-purchase is far less risky than traditional owner-financing deals.

In "low-down" or "no-down" deals, ownership of the property was transferred to the buyer and, if payment was not made, expensive foreclosure procedures had to be followed. However, in a lease-purchase, the seller retains title to the property. And, because the lease is the first part of the agreement, the seller (as landlord) has simple recourse if the buyer (as tenant) does not make timely rent payments.

And eviction is always easier than foreclosure!

If the seller is considering an owner-financing deal when the property closes, he is building a payment history on the buyer during the term of the lease-purchase contract. Obviously, if the payments are made on time and the property is well maintained by the potential buyer, a seller will certainly feel more comfortable holding financing of some type.

On the other hand, if no payment history or "track record" is established (as would be the case in a traditional owner-financed sale) a seller would not have the benefit of such a comfort level in knowing how the buyer would care for the property or honor the payment schedule.

And don't forget that lease-purchase offers additional security to the seller in the form of an up-front cash payment which is non-refundable (unlike a rental security deposit which *is* refundable).

There's also another benefit that many people overlook. With a property occupied by a potential (and probable) buyer who will care for the property far better than any tenant, the seller may have little—or no— minor maintenance expense. A potential buyer will be far more likely to handle the little things that are part of owning (and tending to) a home.

In its simplest form, lease-purchase is a value-added item which works much like a special form of financing. In essence, it is creative financing.

Since the "closing" of a lease-purchase is not actually a closing at all (but rather more like a rental agreement), the seller can have his home occupied and mortgage payments covered . . . and know that he has a buyer ready to pay his asking price.

It all can be accomplished in a single afternoon. Usually without an attorney, without a bank, and without additional expenses.

And the buyers can move in immediately!

Advantages for the landlord

Sure, the seller also will be a landlord for a while . . . so let's look at the benefits of lease-purchase from the landlord's perspective.

Quite simply, a lease-purchase attracts a stronger "tenant."

Compare the typical renter of a single family home versus an apartment renter. Actually, there's very little difference, except that the home renter probably has children and/or needs more room. He doesn't necessarily care more for the home, nor does he feel a sense of ownership or pride in the property.

If you have ever rented an apartment, a car, or stayed in a hotel room, you know what little amount of care is shown by the previous renters. Often, renters feel that the owner or landlord is rich and doesn't really need the income— or doesn't truly care about the item or property.

Too often, renters exhibit their frustrations— higher prices, complaints about service, or any number of reasons—by abusing the rented item.

But that's not true with the lease-purchaser!

In the lease-purchaser's mind, he is truly buying the home. From his perspective, he isn't renting with an option to buy, nor does he think of himself as lease-purchasing. He is simply buying a home using a creative financing method, and it is one that is helping him achieve his dream of owning his own home.

In other words, he thinks of the property as if it were his own.

This sense of ownership means he will take better care of the property than would a typical renter. He may very well cut the grass, care for the shrubs, and keep the place clean. You typically won't receive as many calls for stopped up toilets, or the need to replace broken windows. In fact, the chances are good that those maintenance needs will be taken care of by the lease-purchaser/buyer . . . just as he would tend to the needs of his own home. Which, in a way it is (or will be)!

I have had lease-purchasers paint the interior and exterior of their homes. They've added porches, decks, and gardens.

All while I still held title and they were in the leasing-to-buy stage.

WHY? Simply because they are buying, not renting. Just like when you or I go to the bank and take out a loan to purchase our homes. We are buying that home, not renting it. The difference is that we get title to the home and the lease-purchaser doesn't . . . until closing.

If, at the end of the term, the lease-purchaser can't (or does not wish to) complete the contract, you are still in a wonderful position.

You can renew or extend the agreement by charging another up-front cash option amount, change other terms including price and payments, help them get a new loan, or any one of many other choices that *you* control.

Of course, if you decide to renew or extend the lease agreement, you can charge another up-front option cash amount. However, if the buyer has been paying you on time and taking good care of the property, you might want to think about not charging any more money. The decision is yours.

In essence, your lease-purchase deal becomes a renewal or renewable transaction. You renew it as long as it makes sense to you and is in your best interest.

You can also hold financing. If the payments were paid on time for a year, the odds are strong that they will continue, especially if the buyer has actually bought the home and will be receiving title. You can always put in a strong late penalty for additional security. Or you can get a "quit claim" deed signed to protect yourself.

Whatever you choose to do, it should work for you and your financial situation. If it can work, it represents a good opportunity for you and the buyer.

If you think you might need a lump-sum payment at some point in the future (before the natural term of the loan), you can cover yourself with a balloon clause in your lease-purchase contract. A balloon clause states that the entire amount of the mortgage is due and payable on a certain date. It can be any date you establish and can be renegotiable at that point. Or, you can simply sell the mortgage note to another investor down the road.

Here's an example:

- Let's say you held a 2nd mortgage of $15,000 at 11%, amortized over 30 years with a balloon in 5 years. If you sold the note for cash, you might receive $11,500 for it. This is done many times right at the closing table without having to wait at all for the money in the future.

Another example:

- The sale price is $150,000. The bank requires the buyer to come up with 20% down (or $30,000), but the buyer has only $15,000. If the bank allows it, the seller could hold a 2nd mortgage for the additional $15,000 that the buyer needs to qualify for the loan. Then, the seller could sell that note (the $15,000 2nd) for a discount at closing for maybe $11,500. The deal will close and, although the seller doesn't get all his cash, he gets most of it—and the difference could have been previously negotiated into the purchase price.

Still another choice is to change the terms of the original agreement.

Everything is negotiable if the buyer cannot buy the home and exercise his right or option. The price can be increased, the payment can be increased, or the entire deal can be restructured. You may want to increase everything slightly or decide to leave it the same and roll it over and start the lease-purchase term over again.

Every person's situation is different and must be analyzed individually to make that decision.

If the buyer is not in a position to buy at the end of the term because he does not have enough money, but does have the creditworthiness, you can help him get a new loan. Some banks will allow you to come up with 10% and only make the buyer come up with 10%.

If the buyer is getting an FHA loan, he may not have to come up with any money at all.

Sometimes, closing costs and down payments may be added to the purchase price. This way, the buyer can get the loan and you still get full price. The key is to find out each other's situation and work together to make a deal happen. Circumstances change and, after even one year, may be totally different from the beginning of the lease-purchase.

So it is perfectly acceptable to renegotiate and work out a completely new deal if the first one appears to be no longer working.

The rule? Do whatever works best for you and your lease-purchaser/tenant. Other than that, there are no rules.

The point is that you are in the driver's seat. And, while you drive, the passenger feels that they are driving too! Everyone feels safe and in control.

To me, this is the ideal "win-win" situation. If explained properly to the "tenant/buyer," everyone comes out a winner. Even if the "buyer/lease-purchaser" cannot perform on the contract, he still has choices he would never have if he were simply renting a property.

Another benefit for the landlord is that lease-purchase increases cash flow. When a person is buying a home under a lease-purchase, typically a percentage of the payment goes towards the purchase price, building equity for buyer and seller at the same time.

Also, the landlord can justify a monthly payment that may be higher than standard "rent" and more closely approximates a mortgage payment for the house.

In fact, the closer to the actual amount the buyer or lease-purchaser would be paying if he did buy, the better. I say this because this gives the buyer or lease-purchaser a true experience of payments to see if he can comfortably afford the home prior to closing. This also will help him get used to paying that amount, build it into his monthly budget and, as a result, eliminate difficulties down the road.

A third benefit is the up-front money generated.

How much money do you normally get when you rent a $100,000 home for $800 per month? The first month's rent and an additional amount of $800 for security deposit, which must be returned if the property is adequately maintained during the rental period.

Now consider a lease-purchase, on the same $100,000 home—assuming an $800 per month lease-purchase payment. The option money paid up-front is going to be about $2,000+, or 2% down plus the first month's lease-purchase payment. That amounts to $2,800 instead of $1,600.

And, unlike a security deposit, the $2,000 is non-refundable; it's yours, no matter what.

When it comes right down to it, renting gives away control and occupancy of a $100,000 property for only $1,600. That is crazy!

Why not get a minimum of a few thousand dollars that is not refundable and do away with the security deposit totally? This way the money is yours instantly without potentially having to give it back. No questions asked, no arguments, no courts to go to and no misunderstandings. This process works for the renter as well as for you the landlord.

The fourth benefit is the increased sales price if you are thinking of selling. People buy homes in the same way we buy automobiles. We care about the down payment and the monthly payments. If they are within our comfort zone and affordable to us, we get the car. Often times, we don't even really know what the ultimate sale price is going to be. If we multiplied the payments out, we would be quite surprised by how much we're paying.

When you buy a home, most people do not multiply out their payments to see what the total cost is. If they did, they'd discover that they are paying about three times the original purchase price. If a buyer cannot buy at $150,000 under normal means (getting a new loan), he will never complain about paying $160,000 if he can get it under a lease-purchase and have the opportunity to buy it in one year.

> "I find my lease-option (purchase) residents are super tenants who treat the home as their own. One lease-option (purchase) tenant even paid extra to install wool carpets," says Robert J. Bruss in his Real Estate Q & A article published in the Los Angeles Times on January 5, 1992.

OK. We've seen how lease-purchase benefits the seller/landlord. But it is just as advantageous for the buyer.

Because if it weren't, there would be no deals!

Advantages for the buyer

For the buyer, lease-purchasing is "dream financing."

For no more than an up-front deposit and the monthly payments that a regular lease would require, a lease-purchaser can move into a house that a signed contract has given him an option to buy—and he can enjoy the feelings of "ownership" immediately.

Since no true closing per se will occur, there are no closing costs initially to be paid. (They will, however, need to be paid upon transfer of title at the end of the term if the lease-purchaser decides to buy.)

Best of all, the buyer can move in immediately, without waiting for bank approval.

Many times, people are stuck in the process of transferring to a new area and putting their homes up for sale. When they arrive in their new city, they often must rent an apartment while they wait for their home to sell. Only then do they look for a new home.

With lease-purchase, they are able to move into their ideal home today and close when their original home sells.

For the majority of people, the greatest benefit of lease-purchase boils down to one word:

SAVINGS!

Have you ever tried to actually save money? It's a lot more difficult than most people realize. And the fact is, most people are not very good at it.

As we've seen earlier, we have become a kind of "want it now, need it now, get it now" society. We buy on credit and live from paycheck to paycheck to handle the growing balances on our revolving accounts.

Did you know that the average American has at least eight credit cards? And most of their credit accounts are carrying a pretty hefty balance. That means that most of us are walking a pretty thin line when it comes to our finances.

And that, in turn, means that there's not a great deal left over at the end of the month for savings.

Here's the prevailing American practice when it comes to "savings":

SAVINGS = SAVING to Spend

Think about it. Many people *do* save, but they are saving to spend. On Summer vacation. Or the new Spring wardrobe. Or a new TV for the family room.

It is difficult to accumulate the money necessary to buy a home, even without the normal everyday obstacles that occur—auto repairs, sickness, job changes, appliances on the blink, and so on.

Emergencies (whether real or imagined) always seem to come up, and then something is "needed." When that happens, there goes the savings!

Keep in mind, though, that when you are lease-purchasing, you are in *your* future home. If you are right there, living in your "home" every day, it becomes psychologically easier for you to save for it. Because if you don't, you know that you will have to move your family out!

So lease-purchase is a built-in motivator. It is easier than paying rent to a landlord, then setting another portion aside for your savings account. You are making one payment, and a percentage is automatically going toward the future purchase of your home.

Most buyers consider lease-purchase because they don't have enough of a down payment to qualify for a bank loan. But they are at a point where they are tired of seeing their money disappear on rent each month.

Lease-purchase represents an ideal solution since, in their mind, they are buying the home and can accept a higher-than-normal "rental" payment. Especially since they know a portion is going toward the purchase price.

In most cases, buyers know they cannot save money for a down payment on their own. Thus, lease-purchase gives them a forced savings plan that is building up equity for them.

Price protection is another significant benefit. By signing a contract, the buyer can lock in today's sale price of the property for the duration of the term of the lease-purchase. If the property value increases during the year, the buyer is protected at the lower price. Conversely, if property value decreases, the buyer can exercise his option *not* to buy the property. Either way, he wins.

At the same time, the buyer is building equity in the property with each monthly payment.

In fact, the lease-purchaser will accumulate more equity during the first year through lease-purchase than he would during the first five years of actual home ownership (see the comparison chart on Page 60.)

Example: $800 monthly lease-purchase payment on $100,000 property, with $200 (25%) applied directly toward purchase price—compared to a typical $800 rental or $800 mortgage payment:

	RENT	BUY	L-P
Monthly payment	$ 800	$ 800	$ 800
Cash paid at year end	9,600	9,600	9,600
Equity at year end	0	100	2,400

Lease-purchase: $100,000 sales price; $90,000 mortgage (non-escalating, non-qualifying). $10,000 cash required at closing. The initial deposit of $2,500 is fully applied toward the purchase price; the monthly payment is $800 PITI with $200/month applied toward the purchase price.

At year end: buyers have $4,900 cash to apply to purchase. To close, they may be able to put the remaining $5,100 on a 2nd mortgage held by the seller.

Plus, the lease-purchaser has one year (or the duration of the lease-purchase term) to get together the rest of the down payment that will be required to close on the property.

Lack of a down payment today is the single greatest stumbling block for many prospective purchasers, and not just for homes! (See Chapter 5 for a comparison of rent-to-own and lease-purchase methods used in other markets.)

Since the buyer is required to come up with only a small down payment, lease-purchase provides him with the opportunity of living in the home before actually having to put down a larger amount of cash and make a definite decision whether to buy.

A typical question potential buyers ask themselves is:

"Should I buy, or should I rent?"

The decision whether to buy a home can be a frightening time for many buyers. Too often, buyers look at so many homes they eventually talk themselves out of buying—since they are convinced that they'll never find the ideal home.

So if the buyer is unsure about finances or other emotional concerns, the best answer is to do a combination that offers the best of buying *and* renting: lease-purchase.

A lease-purchase gives the buyer time to get to know the area, the neighborhood, the people, the price, the payments, and the entire deal before actually committing to it. Since the buyer or lease-purchaser has the option (but is not required) to buy, he has the freedom to make a decision which really falls in the middle between renting and purchasing. And he can make that decision in a comfortable time frame, without any pressure.

Of course, lease-purchase offers other security advantages. If the buyer is transferred or wants to move prior to the end of the lease-purchase term, he can sell his interest in the property.

This would require that an assignment provision be agreed to by both buyer and seller. Such a provision typically is included in the lease-purchase contract;

you may want to consult your attorney for specific ap-
plication in your state.

Obviously, many people today are transient. As a
result, they simply don't know how long they'll be living in a particular area before they are required to
move again. Thus, lease-purchase gives them the flexibility to begin building an investment in a property
without actually having to purchase it. . . or even to
know for sure whether they'll be staying in the area.

Instead of throwing money away on rental payments, a lease-purchase deal provides a means for them
to begin accumulating value and wealth immediately.

Still other buyers have a home they need to sell
prior to buying their next home. Often, the bank will
not qualify them for a loan on their new home until the
old home is sold—or they are able to rent it for a price
that covers their mortgage payment.

Lease-purchase gives them a means to get into
their new home *and* find someone for their existing
home!

Example: Joe and Mary Rogers have just been
transferred to Texas from New York State. They put
their home in New York on the market, but it does not
sell before they have to move. They need a home in
Texas, but they can't sell their home in New York. What
choices do they have?

Of course, they can always rent a place in Texas—
unless a bank will approve a home loan despite their
existing loan (and payments) in New York. But that's

not likely; in fact, the majority of people would not qualify for a loan under these circumstances. So, the Rogers must rent until their New York home is sold.

Let's also say that the Rogers are looking for a home to buy in Texas. Most sellers won't agree to a "contingent sale" (meaning the sale is subject to the Rogers selling their old home first). No one can predict how long a home will take to sell; some take months, many take years.

So here's what the Rogers can do.

Rather than moving into a rental property, they sign a lease-purchase contract on the home they really want to buy. As soon as their New York home sells, they can exercise their option to buy the Texas home . . . in which they are already living!

Today, the average length of stay in a home is only 3.2 years. If you figure closing costs and commissions for you to buy and sell, the property would have to appreciate approximately 15 percent for you to just break even when you go to sell. Lease-purchase helps you delay many of those costs. . . and accelerate the equity you are building in the home.

Lease-purchase is that sensible—and that simple.

Advantages for the renter

Lease-purchase from the perspective of the renter is virtually identical to that of the buyer, with one exception: lease-purchase can help you break out of the endless cycle of throwing money away each month for a property you'll never own.

In many cases, you rent because that's all you've ever done. You may not have considered buying a home, because there always were financial barriers that made it seem out of reach.

Or perhaps you were fearful that everything would start to fall apart: the roof starting to leak, the furnace breaking down, and so on.

A lease-purchase will give you time to "get to know" the property. It's much like an engagement period before the wedding; it gives you preparation time.

And remember the most important fact: lease-purchase is opening the door to owning your own home.

Think about it. You're still paying the equivalent of rent, but you know that you are keeping a percentage of everything you pay, in the form of home equity. You are building value in a home.

For once, you are getting something in return for your monthly payment.

At the same time, you are living in a place that, most likely, is far superior to any apartment. It has been better cared for. And you know that you can take better care of it. . . because the better care you give it, the more valuable the home will be for you when you buy it!

Advantages for the real estate agent

Sure, lease-purchase is another form of financing. It won't apply in every situation; some buyers will be in a financial position to simply purchase a home, and some sellers may want to get their selling price in cash immediately.

But lease-purchase represents an additional tool in your arsenal. Even if that's *all* it is, it's a powerful tool.

That's because it *is* an alternative. And it *does* help many sellers and buyers come together when ordinarily they might not.

In other words, it couldn't hurt. And it *could* help, a great deal.

Therefore, it is important for you to understand the lease-purchase concept and have it available should the opportunity present itself.

Lease-purchase deals can be closed quickly and without a great deal of fuss. Using lease-purchase as a negotiating tool, the seller often can get full price—and sometimes more. On the other hand, the buyer is able to get into a home more quickly and more affordably than he would using traditional techniques.

Lease-purchase is particularly attractive as a tool to move hard-to-sell properties (whether that difficulty is caused by the economy, the marketplace, or whatever other reason might come into play). And you will realize your commission when the property actually "closes" between buyer and seller.

(*Note:* in New England, Denver and California, many properties have mortgage amounts far greater than their actual value. Lease-purchase gives you a way to work a seemingly unworkable deal!)

Yes, your commission may be delayed by as much as a year, but think for a minute. If the listing was going to expire. . . and you were not having any luck showing the property, isn't any deal better than no deal at all? Yes, I think so, too!

Usually, lease-purchase deals can be negotiated over the phone. That means no driving prospects around all week looking at house after house after house.

Since a lease-purchase requires so little down, buyers do not have many to choose from. Let the prospective lease-purchaser drive by the outside, if they like it, set a time for them to see the inside with you.

So let's get back to the commission for a minute.

As an agent, you will often make more money on the second sale. In other words, you'll capitalize on the sale to the seller of the home you are listing. If you do not sell your listing, or at least cover the monthly payment, the seller is not going to be able to move into their new home (which may be one you already have listed and, thus, will generate for you a listing and sale commission).

More money is made on the second sale, since this property is often more expensive than the home in which the seller is currently living.

The key is to make a sale.

Since lease-purchase often times frees up a seller to move, it can also lead to a quicker commission.

Getting rid of the first home is the biggest obstacle, and lease-purchase overcomes it.

Robert J. Bruss, author of numerous newspaper articles coast to coast, says this about lease-purchase in his Real Estate Q & A section of the *Los Angeles Times* January 5, 1992: "I've used lease-options (purchase) for over 15 years to buy and sell houses."

It works for him.

It works for me.

It will work for you.

Real estate boards across the country report that an astounding number of agents get into the business and never make much money. As a result, they don't last very long before they become discouraged and quit. That's easy to understand: lack of sales means lack of income.

Lack of income means lack of financial encouragement. Lack of encouragement leads to lack of drive. And lack of drive means lack of sales.

And the cycle continues.

Lease-purchase gives you a way to keep from losing a listing that's about to expire. It can help you salvage a deal (that is about to be re-listed with someone else).

Plus, the agent can negotiate a "fee" for arranging a lease-purchase and collect up-front cash on the deal. Since a lease-purchase is truly two deals in one, you may justify collecting two fees from the transaction.

Many times the seller simply needs his mortgage payment made. If the agent has another home already picked out for the seller and is just waiting for the sale of his home, lease-purchase can help. Banks require many sellers to rent or lease their previous homes instead of making two mortgage payments if the property is not selling.

And qualifying for two mortgages is not easy.

Getting the old home mortgage covered is vital to the purchase of the new home. Thus, the lease-purchase can make it possible for sellers to get what they want before their properties close. The only choices people had before were to rent or to reduce their asking price and terms in order to satisfy the requirements of the bank.

Lease-purchase "listings" can be obtained verbally. There is no need to formalize a lease-purchase listing since it is only going to be used as an alternative means to an end. The key is to get the information and store it until you find a buyer that is looking in that specific area.

A company we consulted with in Queens, New York, Century 21–Best Realty, set up a lease-purchase division.

Best Realty is using lease-purchase literally as a "foot-in-the-door." They are using it to get their agents started by helping them to get an income.

Then, as the agents complete the lease-purchase deals, they find other deals and learn the business.

Since there are no contracts that are necessary to sign, the "listings" are easier to work. Thus success comes quicker and the agents are staying with the company longer.

Best Realty also reported that, during the first two months they implemented their lease-purchase program, they "netted" $35,000.

They're pleased.

Advantages for the investor

Here's the bottom line: lease-purchase is the quickest, simplest, and most inexpensive way to get control of a property.

That is especially true for a project that involves some degree of fixing up. If you have ever tried to go to a bank and get financing for a property that needed work, you quickly discovered that it is nearly impossible.

How, then, do you actually get a loan on a property that needs work? You start by getting an appraisal on the property . . . at which time the bank appraiser documents the work that, in his or her opinion, must be completed prior to closing.

But think about that for a minute.

How do you, the buyer, complete the work if you don't even own the property? Even if you could, why would you? If the closing falls through, you would be out the property *and* the money and time you put into the renovations.

Here's the solution. By negotiating a lease-purchase contract for the "fixer-upper," you are able to immediately gain control of the property—without closing and without the bank. (By control, I mean that you have total access to the property just as if you held actual title.)

Thus, you are in the property, and you are able to complete your rehab and *then* go to the bank for closing. Best of all, you are controlling the rehab work *before* someone else is telling you what to fix or not to fix.

If you want a little extra challenge (and are willing to go for the extra benefit), work out a deal to have the seller hold financing for you while you work on the property; your intention, of course, will be to refinance upon completion of the work.

But remember: today, it's much easier to get a new loan than it is to refinance an existing loan.

That wasn't the case in the '80s, but it is certainly true today.

OK—here are some more options if you are approaching lease-purchase from the perspective of an investor.

If your intent is to buy a property to fix up and turn around and sell (in other words, "flip" the property), lease-purchase represents the fastest and easiest means, since no banks are involved and no closing actually takes place. Thus, you pay no closing costs.

In this case, you make a profit when you sell your contract to buy (reflecting the increased property value) just as you would if you owned the property.

Since a relatively small amount of money, if any, is needed to purchase a home under a lease-purchase, you have the opportunity to invest your money in value-adding renovations . . . or simply to purchase a higher priced home.

Most people get into trouble when they need a large amount of money to put down on the property, and another significant chunk to fix it up. Lease-purchase helps you skip the first issue so you can properly address the second.

A lease-purchase also provides a lucrative way for "would-be" investors to jump into real estate with a simple, first transaction.

You have to realize that, in traditional real estate, the numbers (amount of money needed to buy, fix up, and then sell) represent a narrow margin. As a result, many people are simply scared away from it.

Lease-purchase opens the door to opportunity where such an opportunity might not have existed before.

Example:

Purchase price of a rehab property is $100,000— all cash. Where do you get it, if you can't mortgage the property and use that as security?

Closing costs: $2,500+, including taxes, insurance, attorneys' fees, etc.

Rehab costs: $20,000.

That means you're paying $122,500+ up-front! That's cash, out of your pocket (and that's the worst kind of cash there is)!

And, this is all BEFORE you sell the property and are compensated for your investment.

Your alternative?

Rehab with lease-purchase:

In a lease-purchase transaction, your purchase price is still $100,000. But this time, you're paying $1,000 to $2,000 down.

Rehab costs would still be $20,000.

Your total costs? $22,000 (you see, the only cash out of your pocket covers the fix-up costs). You can then sell the property just as you would under the traditional rehab.

Here's another difference. You would now have only one closing, instead of the two (one to buy and one to sell) in the traditional example.

You'd save substantial costs and would earn a much higher return on the actual dollars you're investing. It's a pretty convincing argument for lease-purchase, isn't it?

If you're interested in investments but you haven't taken the plunge, here's a sensible suggestion: try one lease-purchase deal. Then get a second and a third under your belt. As easy as that, you're in the real estate business, and you have immediately begun generating real income.

And you're a real estate investor!

None of this means you must do only lease-purchases for the rest of your career. In fact, most people use lease-purchase literally as a stepping stone into other investment vehicles.

Across the country, I am constantly talking with people who attend our lectures and forums. Many of them indicate the same thing about real estate investing: they find it very difficult to get started.

Virtually all were unable to do that *first* deal.

You would be amazed to know how many people (or would-be investors) don't even own their own home, and yet they want to start doing "deals." And they struggle.

What's the problem? Quite simply, a transaction has to be understood before it can be repeated. If they have never been through the process of buying their first home, they won't appreciate what they are reading or hearing.

The more I talk with these people, the more obvious the problem—they seem convinced that they need to do a "big" deal first. More often than not, such a deal is too complex and requires too much time (and energy) for the novice to complete. It's just too much to handle—like trying to walk into the major leagues and hit a home run your first time at bat!

To continue with the baseball analogy, all you need to do is "connect with the ball."

In other words, start small. Get on "first base," first.

Make a deal and get some experience under your belt . . . and some cash in your pocket.

You've probably noticed that I keep coming back to the need for you to complete just one deal, then a couple of deals. That's important because, after you've completed a deal or two, your perspective will change. You will understand what I've been telling you.

You will feel entirely different about real estate—and about yourself. You'll know something about buying and selling that you didn't know before. You will have experienced success. . . and success leads to more success!

Be smart.

Get your first home.

And then go make some money.

5

A rose
by any
other name

*No matter what you call it,
lease-purchase plays an important role
in many industries.*

Lease-purchase has been around for some time.

In fact, it has become a well-accepted (and profitable) part of many industries. So before we go any further with lease-purchase in the real estate arena, it would be helpful for you to understand how other industries use their own versions of the lease-purchase concept.

Of course, they don't all call it "lease-purchase."

Some call the technique "lease option." Or "lease-with-purchase option." Or "rent option."

And you have undoubtedly heard of "rent-to-own."

Each term, and each technique, has subtle differences. But the basic principle is the same.

You also may be interested to learn the different reasons why each industry uses this technique . . . and the contrasting motivation from their customer's point of view.

TVs, stereos, furniture . . . they're all rent-to-own!

Aaron's Rent-to-Own is one of the largest and most successful rental and rent-to-own (RTO) businesses in the country. I found it interesting that they're also one of the only public companies in their industry. They also appear to be one business in the RTO industry that is expanding.

Today, Aaron's specializes in electronics, appliances, and furniture. They moved from strictly the rental business to rent-to-own as an addition in the late '80s.

I spoke with a vice president of Aaron's RTO who pointed out that consumer advocates have given the RTO industry a bad name. Why? "Because they feel that customers should not have to pay four times the retail cost of a television. These advocates state, 'If consumers can go to Circuit City and buy a television for $199, it seems unethical to expect them to pay as much as $800 for a comparable TV through an RTO company.'"

On the surface, the consumer advocates may make sense.

In fact, if you think you're comparing apples to apples, you could easily come away with the impression that the RTO industry is taking unfair advantage of customers.

But when you take a closer look at what's really going on in the RTO process, you realize that the consumer advocates are actually comparing apples to oranges. And they are overlooking the obvious service the RTO industry provides to consumers. (And the actual cost is not as extreme as many consumer advocates claim.)

If a person could walk into an electronics store and buy a television using cash or charge, the vast majority would. But what about those who do not have cash and have not established credit (or who have poor credit)?

RTO businesses provide a solution to the needs of a specific group of consumers.

That group is the ever-increasing number of individuals and families that don't have the means to purchase products with cash or credit.

Sure, an RTO business such as Aaron's must address unique inventory and insurance costs that a typical business might not face. And this is reflected in the monthly rent-to-own payment. Still, a person can walk into Aaron's RTO and walk out with a house full of furniture, appliances, and sound equipment . . . and all they need to do is provide five friends as references.

In other words, the RTO industry helps consumers "have it now," even when they can't quite "afford it now."

What I found amazing is the market for this type of business. In fact, the '90s recession introduced an entirely new type of customer to Aaron's: the individual with *too much* credit!

Today there are people with excellent credit but, because they have surpassed a certain ratio of debt to income, they can't qualify for any more. For them, RTO represents a new alternative to credit and financing.

What makes Aaron's even more unique is that they manufacture more than 50% of their own furniture. In fact, that is their specialty—and they are able to pass the savings along to the customer.

Here's another difference. According to Aaron's VP, most RTO companies do their programs on an 18-month cycle. In other words, if you rent a product for 18 months, it's yours. At Aaron's, the same product turns on a 12-month cycle.

RTO started in the early 1970's. Today, the market potential is projected to be limitless. Already, Aaron's RTO is expanding into jewelry. And they are looking into exercise equipment, cellular phones, radar detectors, and even pagers!

Some companies even market tires on a lease plan! It makes sense—if a person needs a tire but doesn't have money or credit, what can they do? Lease!

All these products have one thing in common: they make use of the same concept as lease-purchase.

Eventually, look for the RTO business to take on the appearance of a Sears catalogue. Anything that costs more than $100 will probably be marketed through a lease program. RTO fulfills a financing need that is (and will continue to be) a significant part of today's marketplace.

Let's go fly . . . a LearJet!

The more people I interviewed, the more I realized that the motivation to do leases varies as much as the industries themselves.

Take LearJet, for example.

I spoke with a regional sales manager for LearJet, who told me that 50 percent of their business comes through leasing.

Buyers choose to lease for various reasons, but it all boils down to finances. For example, if a customer leases a plane, it can be directly expensed and doesn't appear on the balance sheet as an asset. That has direct (and more immediate) tax advantages, as opposed to depreciation, which offers a scaled tax benefit.

Expense versus depreciation becomes the driving force for many companies. That's why some companies will lease everything they can. Others will buy everything.

A final note on Learjet. They do not offer in-house leasing. Instead, they refer it to outside sources. Their goal is "to meet the customer's needs."

As you might expect, their high level of service carries with it an upscale price tag. But there's no negotiation; the price is the same whether you buy a plane in Dallas or Atlanta.

However, LearJet will disclose the full price you're paying, whether you lease or purchase.

This may seem like only common sense . . . but you'll realize the significance of that statement when you read about automobile leasing, next.

Have you leased a Ford . . . lately?

The Tefra Act of 1986 introduced sweeping changes in tax laws and, in the process, helped leasing become a powerful (and marketable) sales tool for the automobile industry.

Leasing of automobiles generally falls into two categories: lease with purchase option, or lease-option. Therefore, the consumer has two choices; he can lease with an option to purchase the car at the end of the lease term, or simply lease with no provision to buy.

I interviewed Mr. X, an industry expert and executive with a major automobile leasing firm in Atlanta, Georgia. He told me that consumers voluntarily handicap themselves with ignorance when it comes to buying a new car. "From the day that a new car is manufactured until the day it dies," he pointed out, "it depreciates. Some do it slower than others, but every car depreciates."

That makes sense. If you are looking at a car as an investment, you're missing the point. A car will not last forever. Unless you're going to mothball a car as a museum piece, you will want to drive it. Probably 20,000 miles per year. After that, it becomes a throw-away.

Almost no one keeps a car longer than 10 years. Actually, most cars are designed to last only about 100,000 miles.

Automobile leasing has become a way of life for many Americans; one reason is the price of automobiles themselves.

An average car today commands a price tag of at least $15,000. In many cases, that represents one-half (or more) of a person's annual income.

But wait—it gets worse! Even if they qualify for financing, they are required to make a down payment of 10 to 20 percent. That's one or two thousand dollars that many people simply don't have.

When money is the issue, people are forced to do something else. Leasing is an attractive option, but it always pays to know exactly what you're getting yourself into.

Don't be a "monthly shopper."

"Right now," Mr. X told me, "there is a consumer problem out there. It is ignorance. You need to call at least three different dealerships and compare prices and terms. Don't be a 'monthly payment shopper' or you will get into serious trouble."

He cited this example:

A man walks into a dealership looking for a new car. Leasing is not on his mind at all; he just knows that he can afford around $340 per month for a car.

He sets his sights on a nice $20,000 car. Now, he could beat on the sales staff all day and still not finance a $20,000 car for $340 per month—even if he *is* able to whittle them down to where they're making only $100 gross profit.

Unfortunately, our consumer has tipped his hand by focusing so intently on the monthly payment. So, at the last minute, the salesperson steps back to "negotiate" with the management team, and they say, "OK. It's time to convert."

After a sufficient pause, they send the salesperson back out. "Good news!" he says. "I managed to get you that car for $340 per month and (can you believe your luck?) no down payment!"

The consumer says, "Great! How'd you pull that one off?" And, for the first time, the salesperson mentions "lease". . . except that the consumer really has no idea what that means.

Do you know what just happened?

The consumer spent half the day beating on the sales staff until they had only $100 gross profit left in the vehicle. Then, they go back in and turn his fixation with the $340 monthly payment into a $4-5,000 gross profit on a lease.

And the consumer's head is spinning. All of a sudden, he has his car. He has his monthly payment. His answers are solved, so far as he knows. (Until he tries to trade it in. . . I'll explain what *that* means in a minute.)

Mr. X concludes, "A lot of people leave the dealership without a clue."

More hidden pitfalls.

Automobile manufacturers make leasing parameters appear extremely attractive. Unfortunately, that is not always the case.

Consider what industry experts call the "monopoly money" interest rates available.

Certain manufacturers put on incredible incentives, such as interest rates as low as 1 or 2 percent, to motivate consumers to take their cars. But this creates a two-fold problem. First, an artificially low interest rate can make an expensive car (say, $29,000) available at a price that appears, on the surface, affordable to the average consumer (around $400 per month). So consumers walk into the showroom expecting a deal as good as the ads sound.

That's when the second problem surfaces. Because, in fact, the consumer *can't* get the car at that price. At least, not exactly.

Mr. X showed me a newspaper ad for Range Rover, which informed me that I could lease the Range Rover for $499 per month. "Now," he asked me, "what would you guess to be the price of a Range Rover?" I guessed $40,000. "Actually, $45,000," he said. "That's a '3-bedroom, 2-bath with a fireplace' car, designed for the wealthy."

He went on to tell me that the actual lease on that vehicle is $700 per month. But people see the ad, want the car, and feel that they can afford $499 per month—especially when they're getting such a car!

"But now," Mr. X added, "take a look at the fine print." I looked and didn't see it at first. Then I found it. In addition to the $499 per month, you must come up with $4,000 down as a "capitalized cost reduction."

Why do automobile manufacturers do this? "They are hurting financially and need to sell cars. Some offer 'too good-to-be-true' deals to attract consumers. Unfortunately, it lures a consumer in there who has no business thinking about that particular car in the first place."

But, as bad as that sounds, even that's not the real problem. Because the real headaches don't start until you approach the *end* of the lease.

Pay me now . . . or pay me later.

But what about the consumer who could afford the $4,000 down for a Range Rover and who actually could manage the $499 per month? Mr. X said, "The consumer is told that 'if you want to trade the car as early as two years into the 48-month lease, there's no problem.' Consumers are assured that they can trade the car for a new lease and come out completely unscathed. But that's a fallacy."

He explained that the consumer goes into a dealership and discovers that their payoff amount on the Range Rover is $25,000, yet the vehicle's value is only $15,000. "We call that the Poseidon Adventure: they're literally caught 'upside down' in the lease."

As with most automobile financing, leasing loads a substantial portion of the interest and finance charges up front (that's called the 'rule of 78s'). That also means that, during the same period, the consumer is paying only a small percentage toward the actual purchase price.

Take, for example, a standard 48-month contract.

The average person trades after 27 months; that's a little more than half way through the lease. But look at what has happened: at the end of 27 months, the individual will have paid 76 percent of the interest. So, if you stop the loan at that point and recalculate it backwards to the first day, you'll see that the deal was not what it appeared to be. The consumer actually was paying 30 percent, when he thought he was paying 10 percent interest.

The result is that, if the consumer wishes to trade in the car, he's faced with a disproportionately large amount of the purchase price left, for which he is still responsible.

So here's the bottom line, according to Mr. X. People risk the future for luxury today. They get into a car that is above their means, lease it, get a low payment and then get "nailed" at the end when they go to trade it in or sell it. They never paid enough monthly to reflect the true cost of the vehicle . . . and they'll owe a substantial amount in the years to come.

It's the old axiom, "Pay now or pay later."

When leasing does work.

Contrary to what you might be thinking right about now, leasing actually *is* good for most people.

It is *not* for the individual who is going to drive a car until the wheels fall off. If your trading cycle is more than 10 years, buy the car. If you trade every few years, lease it.

Leasing can help make a car more affordable, especially when your individual or family needs dictate a particular vehicle that commands a higher sticker price (minivans, for example, are not cheap).

The best advice? Know what you are doing!

Leasing is often more stringent than buying a car (or a home, for that matter). And, when you lease an automobile, your insurance liability limits are

mandatory . . . and much higher than the minimum limits required by law.

Further, dealers are not required by law to disclose the price of the car you're leasing. (Read
that sentence again.)

It means you can count on paying a higher price.

Eventually, federal legislation will intervene and
force the industry to disclose the purchase price.
When this happens, leasing will certainly decline,
as dealers will no longer have such an incentive to
lease vehicles.

In short, leasing works best when you know what
you're doing. That's why consumers must become more
educated. You must understand the inherent pros and
cons of leasing. . . and how you can benefit from leasing
as a financing tool.

For assistance, talk with a Certified Vehicle Leasing Executive. Currently, there are about 250 in the
United States.

Certified Vehicle Leasing Executives subscribe to
a stringent code of ethics and focus on educating
their customers before, during, and after a lease
is signed. They also pursue legal action against
false or deceptive advertisers, and dealerships
who follow unlawful or unethical lease practices.

Mr. X says his Atlanta-based company is one that
adheres to those standards of ethics. "Eighty percent of
our business is repeat business. Customers come back,

and that's proof to us that ethics still work in today's marketplace.

"As a professional organization, we try to ask all the questions that a typical dealer might not ask. How many miles are your going to drive? What is your life-style? We try to steer customers toward the car that best fits their needs, that will give them the fewest service problems during the life of their lease. . . so they'll stay in the lease and be satisfied with it."

OK. Let's stop for a second.

We've looked at leasing from all angles. You should understand that lease-purchase is a legitimate tool that works in a diverse number of industries. It is a powerful tool that must be used with discretion.

Most important, you can use lease-purchase to help people . . . and benefit yourself.

Now let's see how you're going to make it happen.

6

How do I buy a home with Lease–Purchase?

The important thing is to get started. . . now!

Every day, prospective home buyers all over the USA are saying, "My dream is to own a home, but I don't have enough cash or credit. What can I do?"

In a few cases people simply might not understand the real estate market; perhaps they actually *can* afford to buy a home, but have never really spoken to someone about it. In these cases, a real estate agent or consultant can help.

But there are people who cannot afford to buy a home. For them, lease-purchase may be the best answer.

Unfortunately, the "I've been saved by real estate!" gurus on television have created a frustrated society of "would-be" buyers. I don't mean to imply that none of their techniques work (some do), but it is not as simple as they often portray.

Remember the lottery example? Sure, you might win big, but what are your chances? You certainly don't want to depend on such a remote chance each week for your livelihood.

Further, some of their techniques *are* effective, but they simply might not fit into your style of doing things. For example, you may not feel comfortable doing a foreclosure or putting pressure on the seller when they are backed against the wall facing bankruptcy.

And, at best, foreclosures require cash. At worst, they are unpleasant and emotionally difficult.

But everyone loves a "deal."

The truth is that, if the average person tries to find a "true deal," the odds are stacked against him in many ways. Experts are tough competition for the few "incredible deals" that may be out there. Everyone wants the big, profitable deals. Therefore, the sheer numbers of people chasing after those deals is amazing.

Let's talk about how to go about lease-purchase to generate some real (and realistic) income. Or to get your first home.

1. Assemble your team.

The first decision is to determine whether you are going to do this alone, with the help of a real estate agent, or with a consultant. (See Chapter 12.)

If you are going to use an agent, you will have to compensate him in some way. If the property you will eventually lease-purchase is listed, the agent will make a commission when you purchase the home at the end of the term.

Or, if the home is a "FSBO" (for sale by owner), there will not be a commission included in the deal. Therefore, you need to arrange some type of reasonable compensation in advance. If the agent is a friend of yours, you should be able to work out something more than reasonable. If the agent is not a friend, ask what they think would be fair. Typically 1%–2% should work out fine. If the home is $50,000 that would equate to $500-$1,000. If the price is $200,000, the fee to the agent would be $2,000.

If you are going to look for deals by yourself, there are many aspects and techniques as well as a thorough understanding of the entire process that you will have to know.

Even if you *do* choose to "go it alone," you should develop a network of contacts through whom you can learn of properties as they become available, and who can help you during the process (I'll get into this more, later). This may include friends, neighbors, business associates . . . and don't forget to subscribe to the local newspaper(s).

2. Start looking for deals.

First of all, you may not be lucky enough just to stumble across a deal.

We have worked in several states where the lease-purchase concept is already widely understood, accepted, and practiced. This means you *can* open your newspaper to the classified section and look under homes "for sale" and "for rent" and you'll find plenty of properties listed as available through lease-purchase or lease-option programs.

> In some cases, the classified ad won't appear as a lease-purchase, but rather as a "lease-option," or "rent-option." This is essentially the same thing . . . just with a different name.

> I like using the word "purchase" in the description of the transaction, as it works subconsciously to drive the deal to close. Remember, if you are "purchasing" the property, you will treat it differently than if you are "optioning" it.

> When you are "optioning" a property, the very term itself implies uncertainty; in other words, you're not sure if you want the deal, and you'll decide later.

> Call the deal a "purchase" and, from the start, put yourself in the frame of mind that you are going to buy the property. It is going to be yours!

In established markets, lease-purchase has been well documented as a beneficial tool. Sellers understand and accept it as a means to move properties, and real estate agents appreciate the flexibility it offers to each party. Even as you read this book, the concept is growing in popularity.

However, there are many areas where lease-purchase has not yet been introduced. In such areas, look for properties for sale or rent. And be prepared to explain the nature of a lease-purchase and its advantages to seller (and/or buyer). Then slowly and carefully guide the potential seller (or buyer) through the process to eliminate any confusion or anxiety.

Since you may have to create a lease-purchase transaction from "scratch," you need to understand exactly what a lease-purchase is and how it works—because if you don't feel comfortable with it, you'll never be able to help someone else feel comfortable.

Refresh your memory by re-reading Chapter 4.

If you want to keep your explanation simple, here's a description in a nutshell:

A lease-purchase is a transaction combining a lease and a purchase contract, in which the buyer (or lease-purchaser) makes payments to the seller of the home. A portion of those monthly payments is credited toward the purchase price of the home—typically, this would be 20 to 25 percent of the monthly lease-purchase payment. In addition, a small amount of money is paid up front—this is called "option money" and is also credited toward the purchase price.

The lease-purchase term is usually for one year, which gives the buyer time to save the necessary

money to put down on a new loan. . . or assume the existing loan.

At the end of the term, the buyer may exercise his option to buy the home. At that point, a normal closing would take place.

If, on the other hand, the buyer chooses not to exercise his option to buy the home, the "option money" is forfeited and all monthly payments go to the seller.

3. How should you hunt?

If you are going to do lease-purchases on your own, you should plan on spending at least two hours a day on the phone.

Clear off a table or desk where you can lay out the newspaper and mark the ads.

Before you start to make calls, determine which ads are worth calling in the first place. Highlight the ads for properties that appeal most to you, or that you feel would most likely be suitable for lease-purchase. Mark these ads with an "A." These will be your hot prospects.

Next, mark the ads that are slightly less appealing, but that you feel could still be good deals. Mark these ads with a "B." These will be your "warm" prospects.

You may choose to categorize the properties as follows:

1A— "for rent" (sellers have already accepted that they're not getting cash, and they may be more receptive to lease-purchase).

A— the ad includes words like "creative," "motivated," or "flexible." You may be able to get a good deal here.

B— the seller has a price focus: "price reduced," "best price," etc.

C— all other properties that may be suitable due to geography, size, etc.

Organization is important. After you mark the ads, cut them out and tape each to a Property Research form (a sample is included at the end of this chapter).

It may be helpful to mark your prospect sheets with a different color pen for each category, or highlight the respective ads with a different color marker— such as yellow for "A," pink for "B," and blue for "C." This will help you visually distinguish the "hot" versus "warm" properties . . . and you'll be able to more quickly make decisions on each.

Now you're ready to begin making calls.

Start with your "A" prospects first. When you've attempted each once, move on to your "B" list. And so on.

Indicate on your Property Research form each day and time you attempt to contact the seller by phone. If you get through to the seller and are able to discuss the property, begin completing the form.

If you are asked to call back at a more convenient time, note on the form when the seller has asked you to call. Then, make sure you call back at that time!

As you are talking with the seller, make notes of any specific items of interest on the back of the form.

Once you have finished completing the form, set it aside. When you have several forms completed, you are ready to begin making comparisons and focusing in on the properties that have the greatest potential for you.

4. What do you say?

You've found the property you think you may want to buy. How do you approach the seller?

Here's the best opening statement that I know. It's actually a question, and it is the one I use. Call the seller in the ad and ask, "Would you be interested in a full-price lease-purchase?"

Then, be quiet. Wait. Listen.

In the next moments of silence, something is happening . . . to your benefit. I would bet that the seller has never heard the words "full price" used with *any* offer for his home. (In fact, when was the last time you heard someone offer full price for *anything*?)

So what just happened? You've caught him off guard. You've immediately separated yourself from all the other potential buyers that have talked to him.

What's the difference? *You* are not negotiating.

As a result, you'll have his undivided attention. He will be all ears and, no matter what mood he is in, he'll want to know more.

Often, the seller's first response will be, "You've got my attention, keep talking." Or he might ask, "What do you mean by 'lease-purchase'?" The odds are, he'll never mention the "full price" part of your question.

No matter how the seller responds, your main goal is to open a line of communication and develop a conversation about the property and the needs of the seller.

And here's where you separate yourself even further from the other potential buyers. Because the sooner you get the seller to start talking, the closer you are to arriving at an agreement and putting together a transaction.

Why is it so important to get the seller to talk?

Most potential deals don't come together for one reason: a lack of real communication. Sellers are bombarded with calls from hopeful investors and buyers who toss out low-ball offers and try to get the property for half price. Some may use pressure. Others simply badger.

In any case, the seller quickly becomes turned off. And when a genuine buyer comes along who is not trying to steal the property, the seller may not be willing to listen to the offer.

Remember that nothing happens without sincere communication. You must convey your purpose and motivation clearly and thoroughly.

Speak slowly.

Take your time.

Do not push.

And when you get the seller to talk, some interesting things happen.

First, you learn about his needs. For example, perhaps he needs cash now. In that case, a lease-purchase won't work. You might say, "If you don't get cash in a few months, may I call you back?"

> There's no need to ask if he'll be willing to do a lease-purchase right then, because it obviously is not the right time for him. This is a "closing" question, and you've just established that this is not the time to close.
>
> If this is the case, only one thing will change the seller's mind: *time.* So use time to your advantage. By asking if you may call him later, you're leaving the door open. The seller will appreciate your professionalism and lack of pressure.

On the other hand, you might discover that he needs a certain amount of money coming in each month. If that's the case, lease-purchase might be the perfect solution.

The more you listen to the seller, the more you can help him meet his needs. And the more you try to meet his needs, the more he'll be willing to meet yours!

It's important to understand the difference in thinking between buyers and sellers. Sellers focus on one thing: PRICE. On the other hand, buyers focus on another: TERMS. (In other words, how much down and how much a month.)

Never confuse the two. When you're talking with a seller, open with a full-price offer, and the seller is already willing to listen. But if you try from the onset to negotiate on price, you will have a more difficult time coming to terms on a lease-purchase.

You should want flexibility in *terms,* not *price.*

When you figure what you will pay if you stay in the home for 30 years, the actual price doesn't matter anyway.

Multiply the payments out sometime. When it's all said and done, you've paid three times the original sale price! It's the interest on the loan that dramatically increases the total expenditure.

Here's an example:

Take a $200,000 loan at 10.5% for 30 years. That's $1,829 per month. Over 12 months, that's $21,948. And over 30 years, that becomes $658,440.

That's $458,440 more than the original $200,000 loan—more than double the original amount, just for interest!

Therefore, don't try to nickel and dime the seller on a few thousand dollars in his asking price. Work on the terms and get what you want with the down payment and monthly payment.

You'll be better off in the long run.

5. Where can you find the best deals?

Everywhere!

You'll have the best success when you talk to people (sellers) who are open to creative financing of some sort. Or those who are more likely to be flexible in their terms and expectations.

You do not have to look for terribly motivated people to make lease-purchase work. *You* can provide the motivation. It's better to find sellers who are more willing to be creative and flexible.

Unfortunately, the late-night TV gurus have polluted the real estate waters with their high-intensity sermons. They have convinced thousands that the way to make a deal is to look for the person who, for one reason or another, is financially backed into a corner; then attack!

That method is not the way to be successful . . . and it never was.

The best approach is to ask the golden question, *"Would you be interested in a full-price lease-purchase?"*

Then wait for the seller's response.

Earlier, I told you to mark (with an "A") those ads that you felt were most likely prospects for lease-purchase. Here are some examples of ads that I would call first:

Must sell 3 bdrm/2 ba colonial
$14,000 down, assume loan
Call 555-0000

927 York Street
No squeaky floors or
cracked walls. Clean
and shiny, ready for
your personal touch.
Best deal in area.
Call 555-000

Fabulous split level. This spacious
new constructon home features
master BR suite, large porch.
Builder will trade. Let's make a deal!
555-0000

New Listing
Wonderful 4 bdrm/3 bath
3000 sq. ft.–owner transferred

HIGH ASSUME! Must sell.
Super starter or retirement, new
carpet, cab, BR, wiring, unocc
since remodeling, gar. $56,900
Aspen Ranch. 555-0000

NON-QUALIFYING. Assumable.
9.5% loan on 3 bdrm, beautifully
landscaped house. PITI $908,
$20,000 down. 555-0000

They sound like they might be flexible . . . at least they are *not* advertising their homes for cash.

Many sellers' ads make it obvious that they are focusing their attention on finding a cash buyer. These are definitely *not* the ones to call first.

But they still might be good deals, so they deserve a "B" rating:

```
JUST REDUCED!
$25,000 off this wonderful
4/2 colonial. See to believe.
555-0000.
```

```
UNDER MARKET.
Call today for this deal.
Will not last long. $79,500
Perfect starter home in
excellent subdivision. 3/2.
555-0000
```

```
1384 Rolling Way
Best deal in town, Ranch.
4/2 with 2-car garage, deck.
$121,000. 555-0000
```

```
Incredible!
Seller says SELL this beautiful
ranch in Livingston area.
Reduced for quick sale. 4/2,
deck, bsmt., FP, 2+car garage.
555-0000
```

And these may be beautiful homes but may not be the best opportunities.

So I'd give these a "C":

```
Only $179,500. Quality
ranch in wonderful neighborhood.
Wood windows, hardwood floors, bsmt.,
2-car garage. Spectacular!
555-0000
```

```
OPEN 1–4 this Sunday.
Spacious 4 bdrm with
ALL the extras.
$250,000. 555-0000
```

```
Gourmet kitchen. 889 Lipton St..
Immaculate 3 bdrm, 2 story.
Must see! $75,000. Best in area.
555-0000
```

```
Need space? Large family?
Perfect 2 story, 4 bdrm,
2 car garage. Oak floors.
$139,900. 555-0000
```

How can you tell what's hot and what's not?

The key is often found in the words used by the ad itself. For example, if you see the following words used in an ad, call them first:

- motivated
- must sell
- lease-purchase
- lease-option
- rent-option
- flexible
- owner financing

- owner transferred
- assumable financing
- creative financing
- negotiable
- special financing
- needs work
- low down

Another place to look for potential lease-purchase properties is the "for rent" section of the paper. In fact, this should be the first place you start. These owners already acknowledge they will not be getting cash for their homes and are only looking for a monthly payment.

But keep in mind that they are simply looking to rent their properties; this does not necessarily mean that they'll want to lease-purchase them.

Therefore, when you call them, their response may be, "I'm not interested in selling, I just want to rent my home."

Or you may find that they just haven't thought about their options. If they're interested to learn more about lease-purchase, use the simple explanation of lease-purchase that you learned . . . and ask them if that makes sense for them.

I've said it before, and I'll say it again. The key to your success is open communication and a clear understanding of the goals all parties bring into the transaction.

The better you understand each other's goals, the better the odds are that you'll come to terms and make a deal.

Of course, the burden is on your shoulders. After all, a "meeting of the minds" is possible only if the concept makes sense and feels right to the seller.

Take your time to explain the details. Make sure the seller understands. Talk at a slow, comfortable pace, There's no need to rush.

Pause for questions. Anticipate concerns he might have and answer them.

Even when you give it your best shot, sometimes the answer will still be "no." When that happens, don't press. Thank the seller and move on.

But before you hang up, ask, "Do you know of anyone else who might be interested in doing a lease-purchase on their home?" You've lost nothing by asking. And, because you've already made the seller comfortable by your no-pressure approach, the chances are good that he'll refer you to someone else, if he knows of an available property.

And here's where your listening pays off. Let's say that the answer was "no" because the seller wanted or needed CASH right now. Ask, "May I call you in a few months, if you don't get a cash deal?" You are leaving the door open for the both of you . . . and the seller will invariably agree.

- You are not asking the seller to commit to a lease-purchase down the road. You are simply letting him know that you're interested, and that you would like to keep in touch. Most important, you are letting him know that his options are still there, if he's unable to get the cash he wants.
- This professional approach will go far to help you develop a good rapport with potential sellers. Should an opportunity develop in the future, they will *want* to do business with you.

Once you have agreed that you'll be in touch, help the seller remember you. Send a follow-up card.

Dear _____ :

This is a reminder that I am interested in your property at _____ .
If you become more flexible on your terms, I would appreciate the chance to talk with you again.

Please call me at 000-0000.

Thank you!

My suggestion is to get these made up at any quick-print or copy center. They can be printed on cardboard stock for mailing, and should not cost much to reproduce.

I would also recommend that you have them printed on a stock color other than white. Use bright yellow, or green, or pink—anything that will stand out and help the seller remember you.

6. How much cash do you need?

Since you are not closing the transaction in the true sense with a bank and a loan, you are not going to need the amount of money typically associated with those closings.

Usually, a reasonable amount down will do. Count on approximately 2 percent as a down payment. Of course, this will vary with each seller, but I've found 2 percent to be a common denominator across the country.

To help you better understand what that translates into, let's look at a few examples of selling prices and the corresponding lease-purchase terms. We'll use samples from different areas of the country to show the varying price ranges and how that affects the numbers.

California—$250,000

Texas—$90,000

Minnesota—$50,000

Connecticut—$150,000

These are all areas in which I have worked.

(Obviously, prices range in every city from very low to extremely high. So, these are simply examples to show price differences, not to display current market conditions.)

CALIFORNIA

Sale Price $250,000
Mortgage payment (existing) $2,000/month
Lease-Purchase with $5,000 down
Monthly payment of $2,000
*$400 per month credited toward purchase price

> *I often hear this question: "What happens if, at the end of the lease-purchase term, the bank will not allow the credit to be applied toward the purchase price?" Actually, this doesn't have to be a problem.

> If you have a buyer who wants to buy and a seller who wants to sell, you can make it work. The simplest way to deal with a bank that won't allow the credit is to not address the issue at all; just work between buyer and seller.

> For example, have the seller pay the credit to the buyer in the form of closing costs. In other words, if you've earned a $2,000 credit, have the seller pay $2,000 of your closing costs (you'll both net the same amount). Or have the $2,000 credit paid to you at closing for "repairs" or "decorator allowance."

Either way, the key is that both parties want the deal to come together; there's always a way to work it out. Be creative and treat each other fairly. Everything else will fall into place.

TEXAS

Sale Price $90,000
Mortgage payment (existing) $793.84/month
Lease-Purchase with $1,500 down
Monthly payment of $800
$150 per month credited toward purchase price

MINNESOTA

Sale Price $50,000
Mortgage payment (existing) $431.33/month
Lease-Purchase with $1,000 down
Monthly payment of $450
$100 per month credited toward purchase price

CONNECTICUT

Sale Price $150,000
Mortgage payment (existing) $1,276.97/month
Lease-Purchase with $3,000 down
Monthly payment of $1,400
$300 per month credited toward purchase price

7. What if I don't have credit?

I am often asked this question: "Can I do a lease-purchase even if I don't have any credit?"

The answer is simple: YES!

However, you will need to have a creative seller who will be willing to hold financing as long as you make your payments on time.

An alternative might be to find a property that has an existing mortgage that can be assumed without qualifying. They are not prevalent, but they do exist.

If you are not in a position to get a loan using conventional means, this is an excellent option.

But creative financing like this does carry a price tag—it's called "perseverance." Expect people to say "no" to you, again and again.

But don't give up. There is always someone out there who is willing to say "yes." You'll just need time and patience to find that person.

There will be ads in your newspaper with information about the types of financing available. Call the ones that appear to offer the most flexibility. Just explain your situation.

Above all, be straightforward. Be honest.

Don't try to pretend that you have good credit and simply want something that is non-qualifying "because you own your own business and don't claim much income."

In today's economy, bankruptcy and bad credit are commonplace. It is no longer something to be ashamed of. (Did you know that Walt Disney went bankrupt seven times before succeeding with his theme park?)

Many top executives and business owners have gone bankrupt—I even went through it, myself!

It only takes a tiny mistake to ruin your credit. And it might surprise you to know just how many people have been (or still are) in this position. Even some of the sellers you talk to!

Remember . . . tell it like it is. There is no excuse for dishonesty.

Besides, you'll shock people by being up-front with them! And they'll open up more because of it.

Place Advertisement Here	

Contact Name _____

Home Phone _____

Work Phone _____

Lease–Purchase Property Research Form

Property Address: _____

City: _____ State: _____ ZIP: _____

Subdivision: _____ Age of home: ____ Style: _____

Currently Vacant / Occupied? _____ Color of house? _____

Bedrooms: _____ # Baths: _____ Sep Liv Rm? Y/N _____ Sep Dng Rm? Y/N _____

Type of Kitchen? _____ Fireplaces: _____

Garage ? Y/N _____ # Cars: _____ Attached? Y/N _____

Other features: _____
_____

Location–Directions: _____
_____

Asking Price: $_____ Trying to sell for how long? _____

How negotiable on the price? _____

1st mortgage—Type: _____ Balance: $_____ Years left: _____

Is it qualifying? Y/N _____ Interest rate: _____% Fixed / ARM? _____

If ARM, what are terms? _____

Monthly payment: $ _____ Includes: (circle)   P   I   T   I

2nd mortgage? Y/N _____ Information: _____

What terms is the seller offering? _____

At end of lease-purchase, what must take place for buyer to take title? _____
_____

Monthly payment needed? $ _____ Amount down needed? $_____

What may we credit toward purchase price? _____

How long may we do lease-purchase? _____

7

Every step you take

*Taking lease-purchase to
the next level. . .
to generate income or to
make your start as an investor*

Up to this point, we've covered the basics of lease-purchase. The "how-to's," if you will.

You understand how lease-purchase benefits participants from each point of view. You know how the lease-purchase technique works and, more important, how to put it into practice for yourself. Today.

I hope you've already started. If so, you're beginning to understand.

That's because the sooner you begin, the sooner you realize that this method *does* work.

With no magic.

No tricks.

Lease-purchase works because it is based on the simple philosophy that you can help yourself by trying to help others, first.

Let me explain, using the following seven points.

1. Winning

Consider most investment methods. They are based on what I call "bluff and parry" techniques that are intended to gain the upper hand at the expense of another.

In other words, one wins. One loses.

But even professional negotiators now say that this approach is not necessary. In fact, it is counterproductive.

Professionals agree that both sides *can* get what they want when they abandon the idea that they are working *against* each other and, instead, are working *with* each other to find a mutually beneficial solution.

But they have to do one thing: communicate.

Effective communication is the foundation of this lease-purchase technique. Listen to what the other party wants. Understand what the other party needs. Then help him find a solution that meets his wants and needs and, at the same time, helps you get what you want.

It's much like rowing a boat.

If you concentrate on just one side (or just your own needs), you'll go around in circles. But when you pull equally for both sides, you'll arrive at your destination.

No, communication doesn't come easy. And too many of us are not good communicators. That's probably because we spend too much time talking and not enough time listening.

Open your ears.

Open your eyes.

Look at a transaction from the other person's point of view. Ask for help in understanding his goals. Then listen to what he has to say.

When you do this, an amazing thing happens.

You start to make deals.

2. Hamburgers versus steaks

Let's talk about probability.

On any given day, more people in this country buy hamburgers than buy steaks. Why?

Price is certainly an issue. Availability is another.

Try to find a hamburger joint. You don't have to go far, right? Just look for the golden arches! And you'll undoubtedly find several more fast food places nearby.

But in the same area, how many steak houses did you see? Perhaps one.

Here's my point.

Lease-purchase helps you focus on small ("hamburger") real estate deals, because they are much more easy to find than the big ("steak") deals. The smaller deals are also simpler and quicker to complete, so you are turning a more immediate profit.

Sure, a large transaction may come along once in a while. When it does, you'll be able to devote the time to complete it . . . because you've built your foundation and income on a steady flow of small deals.

For consistent income and security, small deals are your "bread and butter."

3. People probability

Here's another way to look at it.

Count the number of new apartment buildings in your area. It seems that there are more every day. That's because they are occupied by people who can make monthly payments . . . but who can't afford to buy a home.

They can't afford to buy because they haven't been able to save money.

In fact, you'll find that a majority of people have just a few thousand dollars saved . . . compared to the relatively few people who have *many* thousand dollars saved.

Think about it. More people have fewer dollars.

And even people who are saving aggressively will have two or three thousand dollars saved *long before* they're able to save ten or twenty thousand.

There's the opportunity for lease-purchase.

Quite simply, many more people are candidates for lease-purchase than for buying a home.

If you want to increase your odds, concentrate on where the most people are.

Then match them up with the "hamburger" deals!

4. Batter up

I always dreamed of hitting a home run to win the World Series.

Picture it. Tensing as the pitcher releases a curve ball that hangs, ever so slightly, before it cuts through the strike zone. A crack of the bat and the ball becomes a fading star in the sky. Then it's out of sight and I am trotting around the bases with my cap held high. A perfect Babe Ruth.

I'm just glad I didn't try to make a living hitting home runs!

Did you know that most home run hitters also strike out . . . a lot? That's because they're trying to hit every ball out of the park.

That's like a beginning investor who wants to make a fortune on their first transaction. So they focus on finding the big deals. The home runs.

What typically happens is that they take a huge swing. . . and they miss. Again and again.

Even home run hitters don't start out that way. They have to learn the game. They have to develop a feel for the pitches and discover where they are strong. And where their vulnerabilities lie.

The same is true for investors.

That's why I emphasize trying a small deal first. Just one. This gives you a feel for the "game." You learn the ropes. You gain confidence.

Then, by building on a series of small transactions, you are developing experience at the same time you are creating cash flow.

At some point, you *will* hit a home run. When you do, it's because you learned exactly when and how to swing.

5. Myopia

I've always found this to be an interesting word. It means "shortsightedness," and it is the reason many people wear glasses.

But it also describes the reason why many people give real estate investing a bad name.

"Get rich now." To me, this is nearsightedness in its most harmful form. That's because its practitioners are not interested in value or service . . . just exploitation. They keep looking for "one shot" deals on which they can make a killing (literally), and they give little or no thought to the needs of the other party.

But they're forgetting two things: We hate losing. And we have long memories.

I have seen too many people destroy themselves because they looked for the quick windfall. The shortcuts. They took advantage of relationships. And they manipulated people on whom they were depending for their success!

You've probably heard the old saying, "What goes around, comes around."

At some point, their misdeeds always come back to haunt them.

That's one of the most important reasons I've focused so heavily on lease-purchase, first as a sensible technique for buying, selling, and investing in properties, and second as a form for honest, open communication and mutual benefit.

In lease-purchase, success comes when we turn our attention away from our own desire to make a lot of money (that will happen, in time) and focus instead on the other person.

When we do that, something incredible happens.

People respond. They love it.

And, all of a sudden, they want to help us get what *we* want.

That's just the way we are.

6. What's in a reputation?

As a teenager, I lived about two miles from my high school. Every morning I would hitchhike to school. Every night, I would hitchhike home.

I met hundreds of people along the way. For a few minutes, we'd talk. And in the process, I discovered something that absolutely amazed me.

Every other person I met knew my father. A few worked with him. Some were his friends. Many had heard about him.

And they all thought highly of him.

That taught me the importance of reputation, because my father was an honorable man who put a lot of stock in service.

Dad sold insurance.

But he didn't just *sell*. He *serviced* his clients. And he often demonstrated his commitment to them in remarkable ways.

Dad once brought a check to a man whose house burned down . . . before the man even knew about it.

Isn't that incredible?

The man had been on vacation and returned home to find his home gutted and charred. Dad was waiting for him on the front steps with a check for $10,000 in his hands.

"Here," my Dad told him, "I thought you could use this to get your feet on the ground while we take care of this claim."

Now here's my question for you. Do you think that man remained a loyal customer?

The reputation you establish with your clients will go a long way to build a lasting and profitable business.

7. The profit picture

The final point is that there *is* money to be made in lease-purchase.

Take the following example:

A	B
Seller offers lease-purchase	*You then sublet—lease-purchase to a third party*
$85,000 L/P price $1,000 down on L/P $800 monthly payment $200/mo applied toward purchase price	$100,000 L/P price ($2,500 down on L/P) $1,000 monthly payment $200/mo applied toward purchase price

In this example, the property is slightly under-valued because the seller is motivated to move it. While you may not have the cash or credit to buy, you still have the opportunity to make a little money in it. Here's how:

In the first transaction (A), the owner of the property is willing to lease-purchase his home for $1,000 down and a monthly payment of $800. Of this amount, $200 each month will be applied to the purchase price.

At the end of the one-year term, the seller will hold a second mortgage if the buyer puts down an additional $1,600 to take title. The payment on the second mortgage is $48.26.

A

$85,000.00	lease-purchase price
(1,000.00)	down payment
$84,000.00	
(2,400.00)	% payment applied to purchase price
$81,600.00	
(75,000.00)	assumable 1st mortgage
$6,600.00	
(1,600.00)	cash at end of term for title
$5,000.00	owner takes 2nd mortgage @10%, 20 years = $48.26

You lease-purchase the property in your name.

Then you lease-purchase the property (transaction B) to a third party. (You can do this simply by making sure your contract with the owner includes your right to assign the contract.)

B

$100,000.00	lease-purchase price
(2,500.00)	down payment
$97,500.00	
(2,400.00)	% payment applied to purchase price
$95,100.00	
(75,000.00)	assumable 1st mortgage
$20,100.00	
(2,600.00)	cash at end of term for title
$17,500.00	you take 3rd mortgage @11%, 30 years = $161.90

Your profit will be an immediate $1,500 in cash up-front, plus:

- a monthly income of $200 (over and above the payment you make to the seller),
- an additional $1,000 at the end of the lease-purchase term when the buyer (third party) takes title, and
- monthly cash flow of $161.90 from a third mortgage of $17,500.

You need no money up-front to complete this transaction.

And you don't need to manage the property!

8

Finding the buyers

In Chapter 6, we looked at the lease-purchase process with the idea that you were buying a home. But what if you're trying to sell . . . either for yourself or for another individual?

Obviously, a lease-purchase property does you little good without a buyer. You may know one or two people who are in a position to purchase a home; that's a good place to start. But what about the thousands of people who are looking for homes (or who are trapped in a renting cycle) without enough cash to buy under traditional terms?

Reaching these prospective buyers is simply a matter of getting your name and phone number in front of them.

And you can do that in much the same way as you found properties.

1. Winning Classified Ads

Classified ads are an effective way to reach people who are already looking for properties. You're proof of that, since you've been looking yourself!

Did one ad attract your attention more than another? (If it did, you marked it with an "A," right?) What was it that caught your eye? The location? The terms? Whatever it was, the ad worked. And the more you read ads, the more you understand what appeals to you and what doesn't.

Now use what you've learned to create your own ads.

Here are some sample headlines you can use:

Don't Rent!
Why Rent? Rent-to-Own!
You Can Afford This Home!
Only $1,000 Down!

Run the ads every weekend. You may need to run the ad for only one or two weeks, because you'll end up with more buyers than you can handle. But that's a good problem to have, isn't it?

Run a mix of generic *and* specific ads:

AAA areas	$2,500 down
Norhside	$600/mo
City	$575/mo
East	$800/mo
West	$900/mo
Lease-Purchase: call 555-1234	

```
3 BD/2 BA
$2,000 down
Lease-Purchase
Call 555-1234
```

For how much down payment should you ask? If your:

Property value is:	Ask for:
$50,000	$1,000 down
$100,000	$2,000 down
$200,000	$4,000 down

Obviously, these numbers are just rules of thumb; you have the flexibility to set your own amount. And you'll always get calls from people who have more money and often can arrange or negotiate a much higher down payment.

Several clients have reported incredible responses from their ads.

Recently, I spoke with a gentleman from Fresno, CA who received 60 calls in 6 days from his first ad. A client in Chicago received 35 calls in one week. Another in Denver received more than 100 calls in 2 weeks.

2. Networking

You can always find people to help you sell properties. Your list of "helpers" should include:

- current lease-purchase associates
- Realtors
- apartment bulletin boards (or talk with the managers)
- friends and neighbors
- church notices and bulletin boards
- clubs and organizations

How can they help? Simply by keeping their ears open. Ask them to let you know if they hear of someone who is looking for a property.

But remember, you must be willing to compensate people who send you business. You might send flowers, or take a friend to dinner. People like to help, but they need to feel appreciated. Never forget to thank them in word and deed.

> What's in it for them if you don't share some of the profit? Absolutely nothing! Don't expect people to do you favors and refer business to you . . . unless you're willing to do something for them in return.

3. Listen. Listen. Listen.

Remember how important listening is when you're working with a potential seller? It's equally important when you are working with a buyer.

Above all, understand what the buyer really wants. Focus on the terms, rather than the purchase price. Don't forget: a buyer thinks in terms of money down and monthly payment. Address those concerns and you'll be that much closer to a deal.

How can you find out what a buyer really wants?

Just ask.

Let the buyer know that you have several properties that may fit their needs. Once you find out what they're really looking for, give them the addresses of the properties that match their needs so they can drive by at their leisure.

4. Show and tell.

Never drive potential buyers past the home. Let them go alone. This gives them a chance to see if they like the neighborhood and the exterior of the home. If they're interested, let them call you back; then, you can arrange with the owner for them to see the home.

This is a good idea for two reasons.

First, you must use your time efficiently. You can't afford to spend all day showing houses. Especially since you're an investor, not a Realtor! (Besides, buyers may not like the neighborhood and just drive on by. If you're sitting there waiting for them, they may not bother to stop and tell you.)

Second, you are providing a unique service to these buyers. There may be only a few places where they can get this kind of lease-purchase deal, so you need to stay in charge. Have them come to *you* for appointments.

Over the phone, you might tell the buyers, "Drive by and see if you like the area. If you do, call me and I'll arrange a time for you to see the inside."

Make sure you *are* available to get together once the buyers have seen the property. Meet at your house or office.

This business is emotional and impulsive. So it's important to be ready when they are.

But don't walk them through the home (unless *you* are the seller)! Set this up with the seller, and let him take care of the tour.

If you *do* go to the property with the buyers, walk them through fast. Then, suggest that they walk through themselves while you wait outside. If they decline, they're really not interested (and you won't be wasting your time . . . or theirs). You can then take some time to find out what they didn't like, so you can help them find something closer to their wants and needs.

If the buyers *are* interested, you might ask something like, "Have you moved in, yet?" I've found this to be effective because it is funny . . . but it also gets them thinking about actually moving in.

I've been asked what prevents the seller or buyer from trying to bypass you (and your profit) on the lease-purchase deal. Actually, there's no reason for them to go around you since, as an independent investor, your profit in the transaction does not come at the expense of anyone.

Both buyer and seller need help with the transaction. Because you are there to help, you don't have to worry about someone going around you.

In fact, they need you.

For your help, you are entitled to a small profit; no one complains. They can't simply go to the store and buy a lease-purchase contract—you are part of the link. You are vital and you are compensated by putting the deal together so everyone wins.

5. Why does the buyer need you?

First of all, if you own the home, where else can the buyer go to get into a property for 2 percent down?

But even if you're an investor or a broker, they still need you.

Buyers can't arrange lease-purchase deals themselves. Often, this will be their first purchase, and they don't know what to do or say. And, worse, they think they need as much as $20,000, or 10 to 20 percent down, to do a deal.

On the other side, most owners who have their properties listed as "For Sale By Owner" don't know how to arrange them.

They need help.

Too often, Realtors who are driven by commission will not be willing to help, since a lease-purchase delays their commission for as much as a year.

But your interest is not on a commission. You are providing a valuable benefit to both buyer and seller; for that, you deserve a small amount of profit.

6. How do you collect a profit up-front?

First, understand that your profit is part of the purchase price, so it does not actually cost either party any money.

Negotiate with the seller first. You do this verbally and come to an agreement. Then, fill out the form about the property . . . and match the property with a buyer. You never buy or lease-purchase the property until you know you have it sold to a new buyer/lease-purchaser. The transfer is then done simultaneously.

The process is similar to a standard purchase and sale, except it is done with lease-purchase contracts, instead of purchase contracts.

Remember, if a seller advertises his home for sale at $100,000, he really is expecting only $95,000. Therefore, if you buy it for $98,000 and sell it for $100,000, you make $2,000 in the process. At the same time, you're giving the seller $3,000 more than he was really expecting, and you're giving the buyer the same price he saw listed.

Don't get hung up on who pays your profit. This is a problem in the world of Realtors, who often wrestle over who pays their fee and who represents whom.

As a lease-purchase investor, you represent yourself. If you are talking with the seller, you may say that the buyer pays your profit, since you are able to get him full price.

Think about that. The seller is almost *never* able to sell his home for the original asking price. Most of the time, he must reduce the price by thousands before it sells.

But you are giving him full price. In his mind, then, who is paying you? The buyer!

Of course, when you're talking with the buyer, you may say that the seller is paying your profit, since all the buyer's money is going toward the purchase price.

In reality, both buyer and seller pay. Or, depending on your perspective, neither one pays. I like this way of thinking the best. So do the buyer and seller!

That's why lease-purchase is a good deal for everyone.

Some investors have found it difficult to collect money from the buyer before they actually get the seller to sign and accept the contract. If the buyer is at all hesitant, simply ask the seller to sign the contract with your name as the buyer (with an assignment clause) . . . and then assign the contract to the next buyer.

> To do this, you may need to pay the seller a small option fee (say, $100) until you get the buyer to accept your assignment. If the buyer does not accept it, you simply let the option expire.

> A 24-hour option is all you need if you know the deal is coming together.

> In the lease-purchase contract, just write an addendum stating that you are taking a short-term option for $100, then have the buyer sign it.

In this manner, the seller has already agreed to the sale; you are simply assigning it to the buyer. The buyer won't be concerned about you running off with his money, since the seller's name is on the contract.

We'll address other possible objections in Chapter 10.

9

Case studies

In real estate transactions, fear is the primary reason most people don't actually do deals. If you are not sure what you're doing and you find yourself investing money that you really can't afford to spend, you won't feel comfortable. And your deals won't come together.

Comfort and understanding are the keys to making deals work.

As you'll see in the following examples, our "students" developed a comfort level with lease-purchase techniques; some did it literally overnight. And they all used that understanding to make lease-purchase work for them.

Note: as you will see from our examples, we use conservative numbers. An exception will be the last case in this chapter, a California property with much higher figures.

The following are real life stories. The names of the clients have been changed for this publication.

No cash, no credit?
Lease–Purchase!

John White had been renting homes for years and desperately wanted his own home. He recently moved from New York to Atlanta with his wife and two children.

John owned his own business and didn't take out a large salary. But his store did well and was well-known. He tried several times to get a bank loan, but was repeatedly turned down. Unfortunately, he had two things going against him. He was self employed, and he had made some mistakes in the past that were reflected in a poor credit history.

John went to several credit repair companies and quickly became disillusioned when nothing could be done. He felt he was destined to rent for a long, long time. The only way he could see himself clear was to save up enough money for a down payment and then look for something that was assumable without qualification. It was hard enough to find a home with a freely assumable loan, let alone save the money needed to assume it. (And, since the FHA and VA laws changed, fewer homes were being put up for sale with assumable loans.)

John was driving home one day and decided to take a "long cut," as he sometimes did to look for homes with "for sale" signs. He would then call and try to explain his situation, hoping someone would be able to help.

On this particular day, he happened to see a beautiful little home with a sign out front. The sign said "lease-purchase." John had no idea what that meant, but he knew he liked what he saw. So he quickly wrote down the number and went home to call.

John reached the owner, and soon learned how a lease-purchase would work. It turned out that the owners had already bought another home and were ready to move. Since they had lived in the home for only two years, they had not built up enough equity to sell their home with a Realtor; doing so would have required them to come up with cash to pay the commission.

They had bought their home for $84,000 with a 100 percent VA loan. Now, their home was worth $90,000. So, if they sold it through a Realtor, the commission alone would be $5,400 (6% of the $90,000). That meant they'd realize only $600, before costs! (And since their existing loan was only 2 years old, they had paid only a fraction of the principal balance.)

They decided that the best thing would be to try to sell their home on their own. They had lease-purchased a home a few years back and thought it would be a good way to find a family to move into theirs right away, as they were moving in two weeks and did not want to leave their home empty.

This was a perfect situation for John and his family.

   After seeing the home and loving it, they all agreed on the price and move-in date. John paid the sellers $1,500 down and agreed to pay $850 per month. In turn, the sellers agreed to credit $150 of the monthly payment toward the purchase price.

   This meant that, if John made payments for the length of the 1-year term, he would have a credit of $1,800. Since he paid $1,500 down and would have a credit of $1,800, he only needed to come up with an additional $2,700 in one year to assume the existing loan.

   John received $1,000 back on his taxes and was able to save the balance up over the next 12 months. At the end of the year, John paid the additional money he needed and assumed the VA loan without having to qualify.

   If the loan balance on the property had been lower (for example, around $70,000 instead of $80,000), John would have needed financing in the form of a second mortgage. This way, John would still have been able to buy the home and assume the mortgage. However, with a lower loan amount, John would have needed more cash to assume it . . . and that would mean borrowing it from someone.

   If this were the case, the sellers would be a natural choice; they could have agreed to let John assume the VA loan, and they could have held a second mortgage. This means John would make a first mortgage payment to the bank, and a second mortgage payment to the seller for the difference ($10,000) that he did not have in cash.

Sellers often are able to hold mortgages to make these deals work. Since it's easier to find buyers that can make monthly payments (versus those that are able to make large down payments), many sellers are in a position to assist the buyer with some type of financing.

In this example, John's family was able to get into a home without credit and cash, and the sellers were able to find a suitable family for their home. Lease-purchase provided a mechanism for both parties to come out winning without needing to negotiate back and forth.

When you can't rent, Lease–Purchase!

Ralph Benero owned over 50 properties in Washington, DC. Seven of those properties stood vacant for more than six months. Ralph tried to rent them. He advertised. He networked. No luck.

Then Ralph decided to lease-purchase his vacant properties. In less than two weeks, they were completely occupied.

What made the difference?

For one thing, Ralph offered to credit half of the monthly payment toward the purchase price. Innovative? You bet. Crazy? All his friends thought so!

But Ralph's reasoning was simple. The properties were empty, and he was making the payments himself; the six months of vacancies were eating him alive. So, by crediting half of the monthly payment, he actually wasn't losing anything. He got full price for his homes. He didn't need a real estate agent and, therefore, saved himself thousands of dollars. He simply passed on that savings to the buyers.

Bob Jones faced a similar problem. He lives in Seattle, where he owns a dental lab. Bob had been reading about real estate for years and wanted desperately to buy some rental property. When his friend's mother died and left two homes in the estate, Bob felt this was the time to buy. So he did.

The only problem for Bob was that he found himself with two homes that he couldn't rent. He tried everything, even lowering the payment below what it was costing him. That didn't work either.

One day, Bob read about lease-purchase and decided he would try using it to sell his homes. He ran an ad in the local paper and received over 25 calls. Bob's ad simply said, "$1,000 down, 3 BR, 2BA, lease-purchase."

Bob got full price, his monthly payments were covered, and his homes were occupied in less than one week.

Digging for deals with a lease-purchase shovel.

Chuck Henry was looking for a home for himself, but didn't have a lot of cash. Each week he would go through the classified "for sale" section of his local paper, looking for sellers who appeared motivated. . . or people that didn't need much money down.

But Chuck had a problem worse than cash flow. Because, even when he found an ad that sounded good and would call, the seller would invariably hang up on him.

You see, Chuck is also a real estate agent. And everyone assumed that Chuck was trying to get listings, even though he assured them he was only trying to find a house for his family.

Sure, Chuck could have bought a home that was listed with another agent, but he would have had to share the commission—and that would mean paying the other agent out of his own pocket. That was a hard thing for Chuck to swallow, so he decided to comb the "FSBO's" ("For Sale By Owner") in the paper.

Chuck got lucky one day and was able to explain his situation over the phone to a property owner. The owner turned out to be a wealthy man who did not need immediate cash for the home.

Chuck and the seller agreed on a price. Instead of lease-purchasing it, the seller agreed to $5,000 down and held the entire balance on a first mortgage.

Chuck was surprised to learn that the seller had originally paid cash for the home and, because there was no mortgage, held the title "free and clear."

Chuck was figuring that he would lease-purchase the property for a year or two; this would have given him time to save the cash necessary to put down on the home and get a new loan.

Instead, he stumbled across a truly wonderful deal.

For Chuck, the process of "digging," using lease-purchase as his shovel, helped uncover a property he never would have found if he had been solely looking for "low-down" deals.

Lease-purchase gives an investor the right incentive.

Mike Foster attended one of our lease-purchase workshops that was sponsored by a national real estate group. He told us that he listened to our tapes in the car on his way back home and, by the time he got there, he was so excited he could hardly wait to try out the techniques.

Mike's opportunity came almost immediately. There was a property in his neighborhood that had been for sale for months, but that the owners had been unable to move. Mike called them the very next morning and told them he wanted to lease the house with an option to buy it in 24 months.

The owners agreed to Mike's terms and, at this point, were more than willing to lease the property. In five days, Mike was to give them $2,500 down as option money which would go toward the down payment. He also agreed to pay them $782 per month.

Two days later, Mike sold the option on the property for $3,500. He paid the owners their $2,500 and kept $1,000 for himself. According to Mike, the sellers were happy, the buyers were happy, and he was ecstatic!

In this example, Mike was the buyer and sold his "right to buy" to someone else for a small profit. This is a technique that is particularly exciting since it does not require you to pay any money out of your own pocket. That means no risk and no worries.

The simplicity of this technique makes it ideal for the beginning investor. At the same time, the ability to turn the property so quickly makes it an ideal tool for even the seasoned investor!

Lease-purchase helps novice make his first sale.

It is always interesting to hear from people who have never done a transaction before—and they taste success for the first time. Take Steve Norton, for example.

Too often, people are afraid to get involved in deals because they aren't "experts" and they feel insecure, nervous, and worried.

Steve didn't let the fact that he was no "expert" stop him.

Steve owned two houses that were willed to him when his grandmother died. He tried to rent them for a few months and had no success. He eventually found a buyer for one, but the buyer failed to qualify for a mortgage. So Steve was back on Square One.

After almost six months of vacancies, Steve called us and asked for our lease-purchase information.

Two weeks later, Steve's properties were occupied and he had several thousand dollars in his pocket. He had sold them for full price using lease-purchase. And he did it all on his own.

The most interesting part of this example is that Steve did not know how to put the paperwork together.

You see, there are two parts to a lease-purchase: a lease and a purchase contract. Steve filled out the lease portion, but he forgot about the purchase offer. After we spoke with Steve and he faxed us the agreement, we realized that something was missing.

We asked Steve where the other part of the agreement was located. He asked us what we were talking about.

I faxed Steve a sample contract and he had a good laugh when he realized that he had goofed.

Still, the deal was done successfully.

In fact, all Steve had to do was call the buyers and explain that he had forgotten part of the paperwork. He explained he had never done a lease-purchase deal before. The buyers had no problem with that; actually, they appreciated Steve for being up-front with them and correcting the situation before it became a problem.

In the end, the buyer was happy. The seller was happy.

And, even though Steve didn't know what he was doing, the deal still came together.

The key is not to worry, even if you're not quite sure what to do. Remember the need for honesty. Explain to each party in the transaction what you are trying to do.

Whether you are the buyer, seller, real estate agent or the investor, people will always appreciate genuineness and honesty.

In today's society, these traits are hard to find.

(Above all, remember that if the buyer and seller both want to do the deal, it will come together . . . one way or another.)

"I'll take less!"

Jeff Mason saw an ad in the "For Sale" section of the local newspaper listing a 3-bedroom, 2-bath home.

The ad was written in a way that implied that the seller would be flexible. When Jeff called and asked the seller if he would be interested in a full-price lease-purchase, the person on the other end said, "I'll take less!"

Jeff was a little stunned. He hadn't planned on quite that response.

He was expecting a response like, "What's a lease-purchase?" Or a simple, "No!" But someone actually offering to take less?

Jeff called our office pretty excited, as this was one of the first ads he called. He was looking for a home for his young family; he wanted to get out of renting. For several years, Jeff had tried to save money for a down payment, but had not been successful.

After a few minutes in conversation with the seller, Jeff learned the reason for the seller's willingness. As it turned out, the seller had just completed construction of another home and needed to move in a few weeks. He had tried to sell his residence for almost a year without success.

When Jeff called, the seller was sick and tired of trying to market his home . . . and Jeff's timing turned out to be perfect.

No, this doesn't happen every day. But it *does* happen.

That's why persistence is so important. When you stick to your game plan and keep making the calls and keeping digging for good properties, you'll find the deals.

Chicago Surprise

We were in Chicago last year to hold a lecture and met a gentleman named Harold Barkley. We got to know each other and I explained to Harold how lease-purchase worked.

That night, Harold went home and completed his first transaction!

Harold had been looking at a home for several months and was desperately trying to get the seller to hold financing for him. He did not have enough cash to put down to qualify for a new bank loan, so the deal was not coming together. When Harold learned about lease-purchase, he called the seller and proposed that they use the technique to close the deal.

Since the seller did not need cash immediately, he agreed. Harold arranged a one-year term with a down payment of $4,000. At the end of that year, he would get a new loan and receive title to the home.

For Harold, the price and the terms were perfect. He didn't want someone else to come along and buy the home out from under him. By signing a lease-purchase contract, he no longer had to worry. He was protected with a legal option on the property . . . and no one could take that away.

California dream deal

Al Gardner is an investor in California. His first lease-purchase transaction was very profitable.

Properties on the West coast range from $200,000 and up for a first-time home buyer. (Those of us in the East often wonder how people out there are able to get into home ownership!)

Al found a property worth $275,000, but the seller was willing to sell for $200,000. The seller also was willing to do a lease-purchase with only $5,000 down and payments that would cover his mortgage of $2,500 per month.

Al had a buyer lined up who did not have enough cash to buy one of Al's homes, so Al decided to work a deal on this $275,000 property.

Al signed a lease-purchase contract for the terms on which he and the seller had agreed ($5,000 down, $2,500 per month). Of course, he made sure that the contract included an assignment clause.

Al then lease-purchased the property to *his* buyer for a sale price of $250,000, still $25,000 below market value. The buyer paid $15,000 down and agreed to monthly payments of $3,000.

Al wound up making $10,000 up-front. He is earning $500 per month for the lease-purchase term, and he'll realize another $40,000 if the buyer exercises his option to close the deal.

There's a lesson here.

The key to making transactions happen is to understand the markets, the buyers, and the sellers. As a buyer and investor yourself, you must always think deals through to their eventual conclusion.

This is how Al saw the potential of this deal. And he jumped on it.

He found someone anxious to have his mortgage payments covered and willing to discount the selling price. He met this person's needs.

At the same time, he found someone willing to put $15,000 down and pay $3,000 per month, in return for a 10 percent discount off the property's market value.

Most people try to rush everything they do. Consequently, other parties feel the pressure and they stall. Ultimately, nothing happens.

If you are going to make the decision to transact a deal for a property, you are going to need a certain level of comfort. Comfort with the numbers and the property itself and, just as important, comfort with the people with whom you are dealing.

10

Overcoming objections

*Most objections stem from
either fear or ignorance.
Preparation and communication
can eliminate both.*

In the past several chapters, you've had a chance to see how lease-purchase works. At the same time, you've learned how it can benefit everyone involved.

Still, some people may be hesitant to consider lease-purchase, because the concept is still relatively new. When that happens, you should be prepared to help them alleviate their fears.

Here are some typical objections we've faced in the past . . . and some suggestions on how to respond to them.

When someone has an objection, your first response should always be to ask for clarification. Ask them to help you better understand their needs or concerns.

Ask, "Why do you feel that way?" Or, "How would that help you?" Or simply, "Why's that?"

By asking them to keep talking (rather than jumping in with a quick response), you are letting them know that you are interested. And you are giving them a chance to think through their objection a little more—sometimes their first reaction is an emotional response . . . that they can resolve when they think about it a little longer.

Sure, you may already know the answer. But, in some cases, the question they ask may not be their *real* objection. By probing . . . and by listening . . . you'll help them feel more confident in you, and more comfortable with the deal they're about to make.

Remember, everyone loves to talk about themselves and their situation. The reason most people don't is that they don't think anyone is interested.

Once they realize that you are interested in them, they'll tell you *everything*! You'll find out how they feel about the property, what their immediate or long-term situation is, and more.

Listen and you'll open doors.

When the seller objects
I want more money up-front.

If the seller is asking for several thousand dollars more, your best bet may be to shake hands, say goodbye, and move on to the next prospective seller. On the other hand, if he is merely speaking about one or two thousand dollars more, he is probably a little nervous about the deal and is looking for extra security.

If he is looking for more security to prevent the buyer from moving out before the term expires, respond:

"I can appreciate how you feel. If the buyers were willing to put down only a thousand, I might feel the same way. However, they are giving you $2,500 (or $3,000, or whatever the amount you've agreed on) as a down payment. Remember, this money is not refundable. It's yours. That gives the buyers a big incentive to stay in the property; because the longer they stay, the better a deal this house becomes for them."

(*Note:* you will want to change the wording slightly if *you* are the buyer.)

"And remember that they are building even more equity with each monthly payment they give you. That gives them even more incentive to keep making the payments. As each month goes by, they have more invested . . . and they are more committed."

How do I know they will qualify for a mortgage at the end of the term?

"Of course, there is no way to know for sure. If the people have good credit now and all they need is more time to save up the down-payment, odds are very good that they will qualify."

If the seller is satisfied with that response, stop! Any more might be overkill.

Too often, people out-negotiate themselves in deals and say more than is really necessary, in an effort to "resell" themselves. Don't do it! Just answer what they need to hear.

This is much like the four-year-old child who asks where babies come from. They're not asking for a detailed analysis of human reproduction, complete with photographs and descriptions of body parts. They are happy with the answer, "From heaven." Keep your answer simple and just answer the question . . . if they want to know more, they'll ask!

If the seller persists with this question, assure them that you can have the buyer (or you, if *you* are the buyer) provide a credit report, if they would like to see one.

A credit report usually costs about $15, and the buyer can request one by going to any local credit reporting agency. Or, if you have a friend who is a Realtor or a mortgage broker, ask them to pull one up on their computer. This is easier, faster, and cheaper . . . but remember that the buyer must give you his written permission to have his credit report accessed.

I want cash for my home.

"Of course, we *all* want cash for our homes. That's the ideal case. Unfortunately, that doesn't always happen, especially in today's economy. And when you *are* able to get cash for your home, you often have to discount your selling price to get it."

This might be a good time to find out whether they mean they want immediate cash *or* the full selling price for their home. If they want cash (period!) offer to drop a postcard in the mail to them and follow-up in a month or two in case they change their mind.

On the other hand, if they want full price, continue:

"I am talking about an option that will get you full price for your home. At the same time, it helps you solve an important dilemma: in a market where so few buyers pay full price, what will it take for you to get it? And how long?

"Lease-purchase is a way to ensure that you get full price . . . and it gets someone into your house right away. It's a combination of a lease and a purchase. That means you are protected with the best of both worlds. You keep title to the home while the buyers pay you a monthly rent and an up-front, non-refundable option payment (you can think of it as a security deposit that you get to keep).

"At the end of the lease-purchase contract, the buyers may complete the process of buying your home. At that point, you receive your full price . . . and you've collected a year's rent in the process!"

I need to transfer title to buy my next home.

Remember always to ask, "why's that?" Find out what the seller's specific needs are concerning this property and his next home.

If the seller actually *does* need to transfer title, there is nothing you can do, especially if the property has a qualifying first mortgage on it. If the mortgage is assumable, you may be able to take title and then work out a deal with the seller and a buyer/lease-purchaser.

In many cases, what the seller is really saying is that he needs to ensure that the payment is covered.

"We have found that, in most cases, banks will allow you to qualify for your next home if you sell your home on a lease-purchase and can document that the monthly payment is covered by the lease-purchase payment.

"The best way to find out is to call the bank through which you're getting the loan on your new home. Could you call and check?"

Wait for a response. If the answer is "no," tell the seller you'll check back with him in a few weeks to see if the situation changes. Then, follow up with a postcard in a day or two, then a phone call a couple of weeks later.

You never know what following up will do. And your approach may impress him enough to want to do business with you—if not now, perhaps in the future—because you were professional and not pushy.

How do I know they will not wreck the house?

"May I ask you a question?" (Wait for a "yes" response.)

"If you put down a non-refundable deposit of $2,500 in cash, and were paying $800 per month, would you wreck the house?"

A seller will invariably say, "Of course not." (If he admits that he *would*, that's another problem, and you may not wish to do business with him!) Still, if he persists with his objection, use this reasoning:

"It has been our experience that, when people are concerned about their homes being ruined by the occupants, they are usually thinking about "renters," not "lease-purchasers."

"We've found that, if someone is going to put thousands of dollars down, and make good payments each month, he is not going to abuse a house and lose all that money.

"On the contrary, we've found that the lease-purchasers start taking care of the home as if it were already theirs!"

I want a term shorter than one year.

Usually this objection is stated as a fast emotional response, and is based on no financial reason or motive. Still, ask, "Why's that?" Let them talk.

Perhaps a seller was "burned" by an abusive tenant and is still upset about it. . . and afraid the same problem will return. Or they want everyone else to make up for it.

By letting the seller talk, he will most likely calm himself down and get ready for you to change his mind.

"I can appreciate your wanting a shorter term. We've had clients in the past make a similar request. However, they found that it was very difficult to locate a potential buyer who could save enough money to take title in less than a year.

"Still, I'll make a note that you would like to use a shorter term. Keep in mind that there will be many more potential buyers who want a one-year term. Would you like to consider them?"

If the seller persists with his desire to have a shorter term, put this property on the back burner and move on to the next one.

What if they don't make the payments?

"I can appreciate your concern, and you've raised a valid question. May I ask *you* a question? (Wait for a "yes" response.)

"If you put down $2,500 in cash—that you knew was not refundable—and you knew a portion of your monthly payment was also going to be applied to the purchase price, would you want to jeopardize that?"

Most sellers will see the answer right away and will be ready to move on. However, wait for a response. You may reassure him by saying:

"It has been our experience that people putting more than $1,000 down normally do not have problems with their payments."

If he persists with this concern, point out that he holds the cards:

"Of course, if they start missing payments, they would have to move out, just as any tenant would. And here's where lease-purchase gives you a real advantage. There's no foreclosure, since you still have the title. And the "renters" can't come back at you for any refund, because the contract stipulated that all payments were non-refundable.

"And now your property would be available again. You remember how quickly we filled it the last time; we'll just lease-purchase it again and get you another $1,000 up front . . . plus monthly payments."

What happens if the buyer does not exercise the option at the end of the term?

"If the buyer decides not to purchase the property, you have a couple of options.

"You could allow him to lease-purchase it for another term—this would require that he make another down payment. Or, you could simply ask him to leave at the end of the term—and we can create another lease-purchase transaction with another party."

What happens if they move out before the end of the term?

"That's not likely but, should it happen, you keep the down payment as well as the portion of the monthly rent that went toward the purchase price."

There is no need to go into anything else here. Continue with the conversation as if the question was never asked. If the seller wants more information, explain that the seller has not lost anything . . . that the property can be lease-purchased again to another buyer.

I want a credit check.

If a seller asks for a credit check on you or the buyer, you must honor the request. Poor credit does not necessarily mean that the seller will definitely say "no" to the buyer's offer.

Remember, the seller is trying to sell his house. In today's market, he understands that he will have to be a little more "entrepreneurial" himself! That's why many sellers have moved away from demands for immediate cash and traditional financing, to more "buyer friendly" terms, such as holding financing themselves.

Here's an illustration: I bought a home in New York that was listed for $240,000, cash. The seller told me he needed cash because his family was building a new home and needed the money down.

After the offer went back and forth nine times, the seller agreed to a $175,000 purchase price with only $10,000 down . . . he agreed to hold the balance as a first mortgage, owner financed.

You see? What they say they want and what they are willing to accept are two different things! It's important to keep asking . . . and keep listening!

Just think of the typical weekend garage sale. At the beginning of the sale (Friday or Saturday), a chair might be an antique worth $100. By Sunday evening, it has turned into a piece of junk that the owner is willing to almost give away because he just cleaned out his house and he doesn't want to find a place to store it.

When the buyer/lease-purchaser objects
I want title.

Ask "Why's that?" and wait for their response. Usually this is nothing more than an emotional response.

If the buyer says he doesn't want to rent or lease a home, respond:

> "I can understand how you feel. However, since you're making such a small down payment of only $2,500 in cash, I simply cannot find a seller willing to (or I cannot) give away title with so little security.

> "Remember, we are helping you get into a home that, normally, a person in your situation would not be able to afford. And don't forget that you're not renting any more! You are benefiting with every monthly payment you make.

> "By using lease-purchase, you'll be able to live in your home while you save additional money for the closing."

You can also point out that the lease-purchase contract entitles the buyer to "first rights of refusal" on the title. In other words, he has exclusive right to it if he wants to close at the end of the lease-purchase term. No one can buy it out from under him.

However, if the buyer continues to insist that he must have title, forget it and move on to the next one. You may offer to send a follow-up letter with your card, in case they change their mind (or they become more realistic).

I want the tax benefits.

First, find out why they feel this way; see if there is a genuine reason.

Most people don't really understand the tax benefits from home ownership. Yes, they know that they may be able to deduct on their 1040-A the amount of mortgage interest they pay, but they have never stopped to figure out exactly what they're saving relative to the amount of interest they're paying. Often, it's less than they think.

If the buyer has a legitimate reason (or he is insistent), respond:

> "I can understand how you feel. Unfortunately, the tax laws on residential property do not work the same as with commercial property. You simply can't take the tax benefits if you don't hold title.

> "However, we *can* get you the title (and the tax benefits) if you can come up with more money down. Do you have more money you can put down on the property?"

If the buyer does not have additional funds available, explain that lease-purchase is the best alternative to move you closer to the time you can take title *and* gain the tax benefits.

You may also explain that, during the one-year term, lease-purchase actually helps the buyer put *more* towards the purchase price than he would with a traditional mortgage. (For additional benefits to the buyer, refer to Chapter 4.)

I want more per month going towards the price.

Ask why (you know what he is going to say, but ask anyway). This statement is the same as saying he wants a lower price.

"I can understand how you feel. However, if you really need and want more to go each month toward the purchase price, we will need to pay the seller either a higher down payment or a higher purchase price. Which would you rather do?"

This should stop them in their tracks. It is an instinctive response to ask for more toward the price, just as many people will instinctively say "no" to a question. The only way to know for sure is to get them talking and onto another topic about the house and then see if they come back to it. If you can give them everything else they want (except the percentage they want toward the price), they should not complain.

However, if the buyer insists on a ridiculous amount (i.e. 50%) of his monthly payment applied toward the purchase price, forget it.

Remember to send a follow-up letter and your card in case they come to their senses down the road. But don't waste your time.

I do not want to qualify in one year.

When you ask "Why's that?" you'll find that, in most cases, they feel they won't be able to qualify for a traditional bank loan.

If, in fact, they won't be able to qualify, you can put them into a deal that is non-qualifying or owner-financed.

I don't want to rent a home.

You and I both know that these people are not "renting" when they are in a lease-purchase contract.

It is important that they understand the difference.

Explain that lease-purchasing is a combination of a lease and a purchase contract. It will give them time to save up enough money to take title to the property after the term of their lease agreement. And, instead of throwing rent out the apartment window each month, they are putting their monthly payment to work for them.

11

Unlikely snags

*They rarely, if ever occur.
Still, if you can't avoid one,
you'll find that the solution
is often as simple as
a little common sense.*

Wherever you go (or, more importantly, wherever you *are* in life), you will hear people offer negative advice. More often than not, the subject of their criticism is something about which they know absolutely nothing! This is particularly true if that "something" happens to be new, different, or involves change of any sort.

Lease-purchase falls into that category.

It is unique. It requires a change in thinking. And, as a result, it will certainly attract spirited criticism from naysayers and pessimists.

What do they have against lease-purchase? Nothing that a little education can't cure! Until then, you may expect to be bombarded with their imagined "snags" of lease-purchase. It will serve you well to know in advance some of the issues others may raise; when you're prepared, you'll be more knowledgeable and confident.

1. Lease-purchase is risky.

That may be true. You are taking some risk in using a totally different approach to buy or sell a home. More important, you are taking a risk that you can buy or sell in such a way that all parties get what they want!

Remember what we said in earlier chapters about the importance of openness and honesty in your dealings with others? That also entails some risk.

Let's face it; how many people do you know to be honest? How many people would you trust completely? You are trying to be one of those people, and you are giving others a chance to be honest with you.

That's an exciting challenge. And the rewards of honesty will go far to dissuade the negative preconceptions of "outsiders."

2. You can't arrange a lease-purchase for someone else and receive a fee unless you have a real estate license—"it is illegal."

The law allows you to participate in a transaction as a buyer, and sell or assign your contract to another person for a specific amount of money.

This works the same as a person who has a signed contract to buy a property. If someone comes along before the closing and offers to buy the contract for a certain amount of money, that's OK, as long as the buyer and seller both agree to the change in writing.

The lease-purchase contract must include an assignment clause (which basically states that the buyer may, without the seller's permission, assign or sell the contract to a third party). If it does, there's no reason why the buyer can't assign the contract to someone else. If it doesn't, the buyer must simply ask for the seller's written permission (in essence, this becomes an addendum to the original contract).

Although some states differ slightly in their interpretation, *no license is required* if the original buyer had an intention to buy, but subsequently sells his right to buy (the contract) to someone else. Of course, you should check your local state regulations.

Some people claim this is illegal because they think you are collecting a commission on the property, rather than a profit on the sale.

Everyone is entitled to expect to earn a profit on any sale. You are selling the property; you are simply using the assignment provision to do it before the property closes.

There's another easy answer to this: get a license as a real estate agent.

If you are planning on investing for a long time, a license offers a number of advantages. One of the biggest is that you are entitled to a share of the commission of any houses you help close!

3. The seller may not have clear title.

The best way to find out is the same way you would if the property were closing. Ask an attorney to conduct a title search.

If the seller cannot document his title claim to your satisfaction, you may want to have this looked into before you sign any contracts.

4. The lease-purchasers may not buy the property at the end of their term.

If that's the case, you are entitled to evict the person, just as if they were renting (which, in fact, they are).

I have found that eviction is always the absolute last resort. During the past 10 years, I have only had to evict one family. The rest were cooperative; in fact, I simply went and talked to them. Sometimes I offered them money to move.

Some people hate that idea; they say, "There is no way I am giving money to someone who owes *me* money."

It may seem ridiculous, but it helps get the people out and you usually do not end up with the problem of intentional damage to the property.

You can always renegotiate with the buyer and repeat the lease-purchase with them. Or, you could arrange some type of owner-assisted financing to make the deal work.

The key is that *you* are in charge.

If the buyer moves out and you must do another lease-purchase with another buyer, you will collect another up-front non-refundable amount. I have known several investors who hoped that their people would move out on a regular basis so they could keep getting that up-front payment. They figure if they "roll it over" enough times, they will make more money than if someone stayed in the property for the full term. I guess it's all a matter of perspective!

5. I stay current with my lease-purchase payment, but what if the seller falls behind on his mortgage payment and the bank wants to foreclose?

The best way I know of to handle this, if this seems to be a problem or you think it may become one, is to get copies of canceled checks. Or, you may make the payment directly to the bank for the owner and give him copies of a paid receipt.

You may also arrange for the seller to show you receipt of his deposit or payments.

Whatever you do, it is best to agree to this up-front and include it in the terms of the lease-purchase contract. That will eliminate any confusion and hard feelings down the road.

6. People may have excellent credit today, but tomorrow it could be terrible. What happens if the buyer's credit turns bad and he can't get a mortgage?

This is the same as if the buyer decides not to exercise his option to buy.

As seller, you have some options that include renegotiation, owner financing, bartering (trading something of value other than cash), or simply finding another buyer/lease-purchaser.

7. Potential comparison with "no-money-down" deals.

Unfortunately, anything that is new and unique will automatically be lumped into the category of "no-money-down."

The main difference between the two is that a lease-purchase is a lease contract and a purchase contract stapled together. By contrast, a "no-money-down" deal is an actual closing where the seller gives up his title and security to the buyer of the property and, of course, receives no cash in the process.

It is important to make the distinction that, in a lease-purchase, title does not transfer. Further, the first part of the agreement is a lease, not a closing.

And the seller *does* receive some cash up-front.

8. The title may be good, but there is an encroachment on the property.

If someone raises this objection, it is typically because they are a first-time buyer and simply haven't been exposed to real estate before.

As always, education can alleviate a lot of fears.

An encroachment may mean that the neighbor's fence, or a portion of his driveway or some other structure, is sitting on your prospective property.

Simply get an attorney involved and have under-standings drawn up as to where the actual property line of ownership exists.

This is actually a common occurrence. Often, the neighbors agree to do nothing about it. Sometimes, they agree to move the fence or remove the structure.

Remember, when you have a willing seller and a willing buyer, things can be worked out. A lease-purchase is not negotiated in the same way as a regular closing and purchase. In a lease-purchase, the two parties work to help each other get what they mutually deem as beneficial.

Otherwise, nothing will happen.

9. The owner will not make needed repairs.

The example I hear most often is that the roof is bad and begins leaking during the lease-purchase term.

According to the contract between buyer and seller, the transaction is a lease. It remains a lease until the property is purchased.

Because it is a lease, the seller still is responsible for maintaining the property. If the seller refuses to fix the property, you may have to get an attorney involved. But that rarely, if ever, occurs.

Remember, the seller is as motivated as the buyer to keep the property in good condition. Because a well-maintained home is more likely to be purchased at the end of the lease-purchase term.

10. I haven't saved quite enough to buy the home when it comes time to close.

You will need to contact the seller in advance. Don't wait until you are supposed to close. It will not be appreciated—and the odds are slight that you'll be able to work out some kind of arrangement.

Ask the seller if he could extend the agreement or if he would be willing to hold a small second mortgage. Your best bet is to be up-front (as always) and tell it like it is. If you have taken care of the property and made your payments on time, and if you give plenty of notice, the chances are excellent that help will be there for you.

11. What if I have to miss a payment during the lease-purchase period?

My suggestion is for you to call the seller/owner and, as always, explain your situation. Offer an alternative to the original plan of payments. You may be able to average the amount into the remaining balance of payments. Or you can pay it in installments over a four-week period.

Do not simply make your payment late without an explanation, nor should you simply tell the owner that he is out of luck because you are in financial trouble.

You need to take into consideration that this seller is already helping you get into the home. Therefore, you owe a certain allegiance to him.

Tell it like it is. Explain and then suggest a plan.

12. Should I have the property surveyed before I buy?

It wouldn't hurt. I have never done that myself, but it is a good suggestion.

You will need to come up with several hundred dollars to have the property surveyed prior to closing.

In my experience, I have not had property surveys; so far, I haven't needed one. It's like insurance; how much automobile, homeowner, life, health, and disability insurance do you have? How much have you used? How much do you feel you need?

A survey is helpful if you have property line disputes with a neighbor. Or if you think a structure or fence may be encroaching on your property.

This is a personal decision. Weigh the benefits against the cost.

13. Should I get a lawyer involved?

I will never say NO, but I have never enlisted the help of an attorney until the property was ready to close.

Again, this is like insurance. You will have to decide for yourself how much you're at risk in signing the lease-purchase contract, and how much you can afford to spend to cover that risk.

14. What if the property is worth more at closing than what I am paying for it?

You have a choice to buy it yourself or sell it to someone for a profit—and then buy another home for yourself.

Many people have purchased homes and have seen the property value increase dramatically over a short period.

15. You discover termites while you are there.

You will have a choice.

You can probably get out of the contract if the damage is severe, or you can continue and have the seller correct the problem. In the South, termites are common. They are also controllable. Just because a property has termites, it does not mean you should cancel the deal.

Find out the damage and if they are active. Get the property inspected by a reputable company and then decide once you have all the facts.

12

Where can you go for help?

Help is available to you in many forms. Earlier in this book, we told you to begin developing a network of contacts—people who could help you find (and, perhaps, finance) properties.

That list should include friends and neighbors, business associates, professional contractors, and so on.

Let's look at three other groups in the professional arena that can be of assistance to you:

Real estate agents

Independent investment consultants

The Mentor Group, Inc.

1. Real estate agents

There's no question that real estate agents know the market. They have a good idea what's available . . . or where to look to find out what's available.

Your challenge with this group will be to find an agent who is creative, open-minded, and progressive. As the market evolves, this type of individual will be easier to find. For now, however, you may have to do some digging.

Agents have one handicap. They typically are focused on a commission that is directly related to the sale of the property.

In a lease-purchase, an agent would not be paid until the transaction actually closes. In most cases, closing doesn't take place for a year or two; even then, it is still indefinite.

Most agents simply don't want to wait that long for their commission. However, if you can explain how a lease-purchase deal can benefit the agent (without the commission), he or she can be a valuable resource. (For benefits, see Chapter 4.)

(*Note:* there *are* ways for the agent to receive a commission, or a percentage of the commission, up-front on a lease-purchase transaction.)

As we travel the country teaching individuals how to do lease-purchases, we have found several real estate brokerage companies that are opening lease-purchase offices.

One in particular is Century 21—Best Realty, in Queens, New York.

This company is extremely progressive and readily adaptable to the marketplace. They see two major reasons to do lease-purchases: to provide a much-needed service to their clients; and to provide the agents with immediate income (which helps to retain them much longer).

How do agents generate immediate income? Typically in a lease-purchase, an amount of cash is paid up-front; this is called "option consideration." This amount goes directly to the seller and is credited toward the purchase price if the property closes at the end of the lease-purchase term.

More and more, a portion of the option consideration payment is going to independent investors who are buying and selling homes using lease-purchase. Now, agents can be compensated in the same manner.

Here's a typical example: the purchase price of a home is $150,000. The buyer pays $4,000 as option consideration, of which $2,000 goes to the seller and $2,000 goes to the agent.

Since there are really two contracts (the lease contract and the purchase offer) the agent should actually be paid two separate amounts. He is compensated when he puts the lease-purchase together, and again a year later, when and if the title transfers at the property closing.

(Remember, all parties must agree in writing to any additional compensation.)

This shift in compensation is helping change the attitudes of agents, but that change is slow in coming.

Best Realty is helping to facilitate that change. They are pioneering the lease-purchase from a true brokerage standpoint. They are making it a part of their business to seek out people to do lease-purchase deals.

As they do this, many more deals occur that they never would have known about . . . whether or not they actually use lease-purchase to close the deal.

Buyers who thought they couldn't qualify, or who didn't think they had enough money, are often surprised when they suddenly discover they can actually buy a house today. The public is not educated on financing, costs, procedures, and the many other aspects of real estate that are needed to make deals happen.

Once they sit down with an agent, and find out what is involved, they are often delightfully surprised to learn they are in a position to get a home and just didn't know it!

An agent can call all low-down listings, seller-financing deals, and ask the listing agent, "Would your seller be interested in a full-price lease-purchase?" By doing this, a whole world of possibilities opens up to the consumer that never before existed.

2. Independent investment consultants

These are people who work real estate from the investment side.

They are not real estate agents and, therefore, are not licensed. They buy and sell property either for a living or for additional income.

Perhaps, at one time, these investors rented their properties. Today, they realize that, by lease-purchasing those same properties, their investments are better protected and their income is increased.

If you'd like to work with some investment consultants, let us know. We'll send you a list of contacts in your area.

3. The Mentor Group, Inc.

Lease-purchase is one of the specialties of The Mentor Group, Inc.

We teach individuals, groups, and organizations about this concept which has already proven to offer universal appeal for many different products in the marketplace.

In the next chapter, I'll briefly explain who we are and what we do.

13

"Mentoring"

*A brief look inside
The Mentor Group, Inc.*

The Mentor Group, Inc. is an investment, management, and consulting organization that focuses on corporate and individual consulting, or "mentoring."

Although our corporate headquarters is in Atlanta, Georgia, we work throughout the country with clients in one-on-one or small-group settings.

The Mentor Group was established with the philosophy that most people have never had the chance to talk with a successful millionaire, much less work with one. But that was exactly how I learned—at the hands of my personal mentor, a highly successful businessman and entrepreneur who taught me, supported me, and encouraged me to succeed.

The dictionary defines mentor as, "a trusted counselor or guide."

There is no better way to learn.

As an organization, our focus is to build long-term relationships with our clients. We take pride in seeing them achieve success and achieve personal wealth. And we benefit from the strength and experience they return to us.

If you would like additional information about The Mentor Group, upcoming workshops or consulting opportunities, or if you have comments about this book, we would like to hear from you. Please call our corporate office at 404/936-8060 weekdays, 8:00 a.m. to 6:00 p.m. EST.

Or write:

Ross International
4255 E. Charleston Blvd., Ste. 188
Las Vegas, NV 89104
http://www.rossintl.com
1-800-379-3420 • (702) 547-3640

14

A final word

Now it's your turn.

When asked why they *don't* try something new, people cite one reason more than all others combined: fear of the unknown.

It is that fear that prevents many people from benefiting from real estate—whether it's owning their own home, or investing in real estate as a way to generate income and wealth.

But information and understanding dispel that fear.

You now have the information. But you also have a perspective and understanding of lease-purchase that I have cultivated and refined over many years.

I want to thank you for spending time with this book. I hope it was educational first, and entertaining second. And I hope you'll read it again. Often.

Now it's your turn.

Take this information and make something happen.

Don't let indecision hold you back any longer. There are a lot of people out there who are ready and willing to help you.

To borrow a catch advertising phrase from a famous athletic shoemaker,

"Just do it!"